My Gaze Is Turned Inward

MY GAZE IS TURNED INWARD

Letters, 1934–1943

GERTRUD KOLMAR

Edited and with an afterword by Johanna Woltmann
Translated from the German and with a preface by Brigitte M. Goldstein

NORTHWESTERN UNIVERSITY PRESS
Evanston, Illinois

Northwestern University Press
Evanston, Illinois 60208-4170

Printed in the United States of America

10 9 8 7 6 5 4 3 2 1

ISBN 0-8101-1854-8 (cloth)
ISBN 0-8101-1855-6 (paper)

Library of Congress Cataloging-in-Publication data are available
from the Library of Congress.

❖

Contents

❀

Translator's Preface

Gertrud Kolmar's letters and postcards, written between the fall of 1938 and early 1943, to her sister Hilde and other family members read like a sequential personal story within the wider events that will ultimately destroy her life together with Jewish life in Europe. This is the story of a woman facing what she increasingly comes to regard as her unalterable fate. It contains all the tragic elements of an individual in the grip of an overwhelming adversarial power whose murderous scheme she is powerless to escape in the end. The path that leads toward "the end" becomes ever more narrow and constricting, marked by a pariah existence. It is littered with deprivation, humiliation, forced labor, and myriad prohibitions meant to embitter the lives of the Jews. The oppressor is never mentioned by name in the letters. Neither is there any direct reference to the Nazi excesses such as the pogrom of November 1938; conscription into forced labor; the day-to-day harassment, humiliations, and injustices; compulsory wearing of the *Judenstern* (Jewish star), limiting of rations and of the time when Jews could buy food; and the mass deportations from Berlin to the East, beginning in September/October 1941. No mention of this, which must have affected her profoundly, is to be found in these letters, except in veiled hints. When her father, Ludwig Chodziesner, is taken away to Theresienstadt (she did not know the destination), she speaks in coded words of his departure. The reasons for this circumspection are clear—the fear of Nazi censorship that might cut her off completely from the loved ones abroad. Since all Jews had to add the name "Israel" or "Sara" to their given names, the censor could easily identify the letter writer as Jewish.

The letters give a glimpse into the inner life of the poet, who gradually comes to terms with the hostile outer world by withdrawing within herself. In May 1939, she describes a walk through the area where she was living in Berlin: "I try very hard to relate somehow to my local, landscapeless surroundings, but to no avail. . . . Suddenly I noticed, somewhat baffled, that unlike my usual habit, I did not look at the houses, the shops, the people I met. 'You must keep your eyes peeled, be vigilant,' I commanded myself. Good. Five minutes later, again I stopped seeing, my gaze was turned inward again like a day-dreaming, inattentive pupil in a classroom." She describes herself as a "stranger" and blames it on the "impersonal, sterile atmosphere" of the area. We can presume that she was not only shutting out the unap-pealing physical aspects of the big city but also the human world that had ostracized her and made her a stranger in the city of her birth.

In some ironic way, the omission of detailed graphic descriptions of acts of violence and humiliation, which she no doubt witnessed and endured herself, benefits the narrative of the letters insofar as the focus is on her private world and draws a connecting line to her poetic work. These are not eyewitness accounts to terror, nor are they meant to be, as are the diaries of Victor Klemperer or the notebooks of Oskar Rosen-feld from the Łódź ghetto, and the various accounts by inhabitants of ghettos in Poland, which specifically aimed to let the world know what was happening. Yet, we feel in Gertrud Kolmar's very private, in-timate dialogues the intensifying terror even as she reminisces about events in the past. A chilled quietude overcomes the reader as Kolmar reaches out, ending several of the letters to her sister with "I hold your hand in mine."

In these letters, the poet opens herself up, revealing her innermost thoughts as she had never done before. Here she frequently refers to her poetry—she is fully conscious that she is a poet of extraordinary gifts—with which her sister is familiar, and invokes events in the past that had inspired her to write. Gertrud Kolmar was endowed with a rich imagination and created a world into which she retreated, but the initial spark came mostly from reality.

In connection with her sister's expressed desire for a fulfilling occu-pation outside the home, she writes on May 15, 1939: "As for myself, I am made of a very different mold and presumably would have dedi-cated myself to household and raising children without missing out on anything. And, believe me, without becoming superficial and shallow in the process. No, for me these simple, everyday things would have had a different, deeper meaning than they have for most women. My calling always rested quietly *in* me, and there it remains, and what I am seeking is a suitable setting in which to dedicate myself to it. And I don't know . . . somehow I always thought that this suitable setting could not be found in America. I cannot get around the fact that my face is—as in our prayer—always turned toward the East. . . ."

Here she reiterates several themes that recur in much of her poetry: the longing for a child, for permanent love, and for the East, by which she understands all lands east of Germany, including Russia, Asia, and the Middle East, specifically Palestine. Her longing for the East is expressed in an idealized picture of some unnamed area in the poem "Farewell."

Eastward I am sending my face:
I want to take it off.
May it remain there in the light
And rest a little while

From my gaze onto the world,
From my gaze onto myself,
The massive wall of daily gain
The driving wheel of go-make-haste.

The world, it carries in red and gray
Through rubble's lament and smoke
The chosen, mere drops of dew on a sheaf of wheat,
A glittering, fleeting course of life,
The shaking of a mighty hand:
Some devoured the midday,
The others swallowed the sand.

Therefore I shall be gay and still,
When my work is done,
In a thousand rivulets
I'll be running with the swan,
Who's without speech and noisy blare
And likely without thought,
A creature mute, a creature fair,
Neither spirit nor symbol.

And when a mere soft splash I'll be
Against shores of pallid gray,
I'll roll out one early winter day,
Eternal death's sarcophag, silvery and cool,
Wherein my face rests airy light
      like spider's weave,
Fluttering gently with a fading smile,
And drifting away without pain.

In a letter of July 14, 1940, Gertrud Kolmar chats about some of the books she was reading that touched her most deeply. She found inspiration and solace particularly in the letters and verses of Rainer Maria Rilke. In the course of this discussion, she relates how she came to write one of her most beautiful poems, inspired by the title of a book she once bought that had turned out to be disappointing.

OUT OF THE DARKNESS

Out of the darkness I come, a woman,
I carry a child but no longer know whose;
Once I knew it.
But now no man is for me anymore. . . .
They all have trickled away like rivulets,
Gulped up by the earth.
I continue on my way.
For I want to reach the mountains before daybreak,
and the stars are beginning to fade.

Out of the darkness I come.
Through dusky alleys I wandered alone,
When, suddenly, a charging light's talons tore the soft blackness,
The wild cat, the hind,
And doors flung open wide, disgorged ugly screams, wild howls,
      beastly roar.
Drunkards wallowed. . . .
I shook all this from the hem of my dress along the way.

I traversed the deserted marketplace.
Leaves floated in puddles, reflecting the moon.

Haggard, hungry dogs sniffed the refuse on the cobblestones.
Trampled fruit rotted away,
And an old man in rags tormented wretched strings with his play
And sang with a thin, discordant, plaintive voice
Unheard.
Once, these fruits ripened in sun and dew,
Dreaming still of the fragrance and bliss of the loving bloom,
But the wailing beggar
Had long forgotten and knew nothing but hunger and thirst.

Before the castle of the mighty I halted,
And as I set foot on the lowest step,
The flesh-red porphyry burst creaking under my sole.—
I turned
And looked up at the plain window, the late candle of the thinker,
He pondered and pondered, never finding his query's resolve.
And to the shaded little lamp of the infirm, who still did not learn,
How he should die.
Under the arch of the bridge,
Two ghastly skeletons fought over gold.
I lifted up my poverty as a gray shield before my face
And passed unimperiled.

Far off, the river speaks with its banks.

Now, I struggle along a rocky, cumbersome path.
Fallen rocks, thorny bushes wound my blind, searching hands:
A cave awaits,
Its deepest chasm a shelter for the metal-green raven
    who has no name.
There I shall enter,
Under the aegis of those huge, shadowing wings, I shall
    crouch down and rest.
Somnolent, I shall listen to my child's mute, growing word,
And sleep, my face turned toward the East, until sunrise.

On the subject of a sudden turning toward religious observance and prayer, from which even her father was not immune, Gertrud Kolmar expresses almost cynical skepticism. Thus she comments in the letter

of August 8, 1942: "For modern man—in other times, it may have
been different—nothing is probably more difficult than true prayer as
distinct from mere repetition of formulas. Do you know when I prayed
most fervently? Not when I was unhappy . . . I heard the deep breathing of the slumberer next to me at night. And I reached out with my
hand without touching him, and I saw on the ceiling a blackish blue sky
with singing golden stars. And I sat up in my bed, and I prayed. . . ."
The same theme is found in poetic form in "Barren."

> The women of the West do not wear the veil.
> The women of the East take it off.
> I want to shroud my face in a dark veil;
> For it is no longer beautiful to behold, no longer
>   lovely, for it is gray and bears fissures
>   like the brittle stones in a cold hearth.
> My hair dusts ashes.
>
> This is the way I want to wait alone in the dusk on a narrow,
>   high-back bench,
> This is the way I want to sit there as night slowly descends around me,
> A black veil.
> I draw it around me and cover my face.
>
> But my eyes stare. . . .
>
> I see. I feel:
> Through the locked door enters quietly a child.
> The only one destined for me and I did not bear.
> Did not bear for the sake of my sin; God is just.
> I remain silent, without murmur, I carry and bury
>   my head, and thus I may search for him
> On many a night.
>
> A lad.
> Only this one: tender, mute, and pleading, with soft
>   dark curls,
> Under the brownish brow, the strange, gray green sea eyes
>   of the one I loved, whom I will always love.
> He fears me not, does not retreat trembling from the caresses

of my wilted lips and hands.
He nears, and his blue velvet touches my arm, his
    playful little fingers reach for my soul
And hurt it.
Sometimes he brings me his marbles, dark, gold-veined,
    called tiger eyes,
Or then again a flower, a pale narcissus,
Or a seashell, with reddish knobs; he lifts it gently to my ear,
    and I listen to the rushing inside.

Once
About the half night, a winter night,
I awoke and peered through the shadows:
The one who loved me, rested on my bed, sleeping.
His breath was rushing seashells in the stillness. . . .
He slumbered deep, sheltered in my love
Under dreams: they folded their wings over him, purple like
    the juice of the silky pomegranate we shared.
Peace.
And I was happy and rose and sat up, praying fervently,
And again lowered my head and held it in my hands, and
    stammered thanks upon thanks.
From my blood
Bloomed the rose. . . .

This was the seed night,
The night of an unwhispered plea, asking to be blessed,
    but I conceived you not.
See your mother weep. . . .
You too will die.
On the morrow I shall take a spade, go under the snowberry bushes, and
    bury you. . . .

As time passes, the letters focus more and more on memories of the past, on moments of pleasure the poet had experienced in her life. In the last letter, of February 21, 1943, she recalls again her stay in Hamburg many years before and indicates that it was this city she had in mind when she wrote the poem "Die Stadt."

THE CITY

They wandered
Through the misty cool winter morn, lovers,
    hand in hand.
Under their soles the ground crumbled hard, frozen puddles
    shattered like glass.

Down by the riverbank
Someone in brown velvet vest sat by his easel,
Painted the leafless, drooping willow.
Curious children were stealing closer,
And grown-ups on errands halted for a moment,
    scorned and praised.
On the algae-green, slippery crossway
Floated a leaking, broken-down boat.
Three swans on the wave
Were bending their stem-slender necks, silent, unfolding, blossomed.
The woman broke bread and tossed it far into the waters.

Under gaping oaks,
Branches black, contorted, as if raising their martyred limbs,
They stepped on the frost overlain grass, wild ivy-covered pillars of
    closed gardens.
When they reached the long, stone bridge,
The sun was tearing the fog like a garment,
And the city rose slanting behind the expansive riverbed.
Rooftops stacked above and next to each other, gleaming black gray
    like raven feathers, some higher up of
    patina green; sparkling towering golden caps.
Seagulls circled cawing, hungry fluttering beggars, about the bridge
    railing.
They crossed over it
And watched the boys in front of squat, ordinary houses, bandaging
    their yellow dog's injured paw.
Women carrying shopping nets, handle baskets, casting a suspicious look
    at the idle strangers as they hurried by,
Disappeared behind the doors of dusky little shops.

The streets began to get louder and stronger, wealthier and more plentiful.
Stately inns beckoned with bright letters;
Reddish brick walls stood erect, powerful, eminent like
    magistrates of olden days in puffy doublets, caps, and resplendent gowns.
Trains made gleeful noises, ringing nimbly like a street urchin at the
        park gate,
    and ducked away.
Men in heavy, warm overcoats conferred, smoking and walking briskly,
    about trade and exchange.
Soon the food vendors' stands began to waft their delicious cooking
        smells.
Shop followed shop,
Offering tender, juicy meat and venison, fish, smoked eel and sprats,
Offering crispy, brown, elongated bread, sweet, filled with corinths, and
    a coarse kind, dusted with flour and sprinkled with salt and caraway
        seeds.
Between two copper cups a tiny Chinese teahouse of cherry red lacquered
    wood cowered its curved, gilded roof.
But the vaulted lair, where for dear money potions and salves
    and powders are mixed and administered,
Showed through its window an old man, as if alive, leaning in a chair,
In a woolen garb, with a snow white, flowing beard;
He closed his eyes.
Behind him grinning a tall, ghastly skeleton with scornful
    eye sockets and teeth of a skull.
The gleaming sickle in one hand and clawing the sinking man's shoulder
    with the other.
A clock struck midnight.
The startled woman reached for the man—

But he nodded and smiled;
For all he saw was her dark hair and her pale, dark-eyed face.

A remarkable aspect of Gertrud Kolmar's letters is her growing acceptance of what she calls her "fate." She found confirmation of the "positive" attitude with which she decided to approach the yoke (for instance, the factory work) imposed on her in Spinoza's concept of

freedom of the human will in the midst of unfreedom. She writes on
December 15, 1942: "For it was not up to me to accept or reject this
factory work . . . ; I had to acquiesce and carry it out. But I was free in
my inner soul to adopt a negative or a positive attitude toward it, to approach it willingly or unwillingly. At the moment when I *affirmed* it in
my heart, the pressure was lifted. . . . In this way I was free in the midst
of my unfreedom." From there she looks toward the future and how she
will face the unknown. "This is how I want to walk under my fate, may
it be as tall as a tower, may it be as black and oppressive as a cloud. Even
though I don't know it yet: I have affirmed it in advance; I have surrendered to it in advance, and therefore, I know that it will not crush me;
it will not find me meek and small." *Amor fati*—love of fate—is the
poet's way of facing the fate she knows she is powerless to avert whatever form it may take. On January 24, 1943, she confirms this as a lesson she had learned in life but also as something that was always part of
her: "The seed of this was, I believe, always in me, maybe already as a
green shoot; but only now is it flowering and bursting forth. . . ." This
was also the bond to which she clung as a Jew to the martyrs of her
people who had gone to pillar and stake in centuries before.

One may argue that it was naive of her to think that she could anticipate anything like Auschwitz. But this is a moot point—nobody
could anticipate that unimaginable hell. The fact is that Gertrud Kolmar was not misled about the ultimately murderous designs of the en-
emy. Striking, therefore, is a poem, she wrote in 1933 that betrays an
uncanny prescience.

IN THE CAMP

Those who go about here are mere corpses
They no longer have a soul,
Are mere names in the books of the scriveners,
Prisoners: men, women, and boys,
Their eyes are empty and void.

With crumbling, broken look
At the hours, as in a dark hole
Strangled, trampled, beaten blind
Their torment's moan, mad with terror,
A beast, crawling on hands and feet . . .

They still have ears to hear
But nevermore their own anguished scream.
Prison cells close in, destroy:
No heart, no heart left to protest!
The soft alarm rips shrill.

They labor dull, gray, not themselves,
Cut off from bustling human life,
Petrified, branded, marked with lashes,
Like cattle waiting for the butcher's knife
And dimly recognize hurdle and trough.

Only fear, only fear in their mien,
When at night a shot its victim seeks . . .
And to none appeared the man,
Who silently among them
Carries his barren cross to the executioner's block.

Death, acceptance of its inevitability, is a frequent theme in Gertrud Kolmar's poetry. She often spoke about her mortality and saw her own death as a liberation, a return home, as in the poem "Heimweh."

LONGING TO GO HOME

Why should I not want to die today?
Someday I shall have to go.
My days, my years are rolling
Downhill toward the seas,
Where grayish fishes silence sing,
Nibbling-soft and gilded speech,
Swaying viper breaks its muted flute
From scaly rings.

A gentle breeze lingers on my cheeks,
A song still on my lips,
My eyes have taken the path
That leads away from life,
From the town that with curvéd light
Sharply mows the soft, dark night,
Spurning with scowling, frenzied faces,
All tidings whispered softly in its ear.

This, my own face, I would like to hold,
As it overflows with words,
Would like to lower it, fold it in quietly,
Like the flower, the calyx,
Until no more harsh scorn of stone
Is heard nor drivel or filth,
Only a dew, a child's soft sobs,
Float through the blossom's glow.

With beggar's pan in hand old age staggers on,
Shivering, over barren desert land;
Deep into the red sound of the fire butterfly,
Into the meadow's greenish script,
I want to sink and rest, abandoned still,
Where the temple vanished at the water's edge:
Dust and sometimes shun the wave
Under the head like a hand.

Gertrud Kolmar's poetic work is an effusion of imagery, allusions, suffused with brilliant colors and exotic fragrances. It teems with animals and plants, gemstones and metals, and a parade of eccentric characters, mostly women at the margins of society. A masterful painter of scenes, of settings, sometimes in painstaking detail, often in splashed brush strokes, she is above all a storyteller. Almost all of her poems are molds of plot, development, settings, and a distinct mood for her to pour, in virtuosic language, her soul's emotions, longings, sensations. She took her inspiration not only from legends, history, and the Bible but also from something as mundane as a series of pictures of German town coats of arms put out by a popular brand of coffee, from which she created literary masterpieces. But most of all, her inspiration came from life, from her experiences, from her world close to nature and her beloved animals. As she mentions several times in the letters, the separation from her borzoi, Flora, was especially painful to her. This type of dog figures in several of her writings. The poem "Borzoi" expresses her closeness to the animal and nature, both lost irretrievably when she was forced to move to the city.

Yours was the darkness, the cave of the mother's womb.
Yours was the ground, the earth, that carried the beasts.

Blind, you groped about, searching, sucking under the tits of the she-dog.
Nursing, you grew and became seeing
And played among siblings. . . .
Do you remember?
No, you don't remember anything.
You hardly know the coat flowing about you, white flakes, a foaming sea
    girding grayish green isles.

You, lovely, graceful one, of narrow, elongated head and gentle, gleaming
    brown almond eyes.
You dream
Northern, pale beech trees in the moss from which rises a blackish fiery
        monster,
        the trowel-horned elk;
Your blood
Still chases after the gray wolf through the pine darkness of Russian
        forests,
Still tracks grazing reindeer herds across the tundra's lichen and moss,
Still hears the moaning lament of ice rabbit
Fearful of hunger. . . .

In the daytime
You rest quietly on your blanket, lifting your feminine face toward me with
    the gentleness of the hind, the unicorn,
Or you wander around, head lowered, sniffing and scraping at the refuse
        pile,
    bushes, and flower beds, the way dogs do.

On autumn nights
When the stars flicker bright and cold,
And here and there the sound is heard of a drop falling from a tree,
When yellowed grass breathes fresh, damp air,
I put my coat over my shoulders, open the iron gate of the garden;
You storm out, with leaps and bounds.
You fly, you whirl up
Like a snowstorm over the carpet of wilted, wet leaves;
Silvery flowing flame, your furry tail blazing after you.
I walk along, calling to you in a hushed voice, and you wait, tall and light,
    a specter at the road's bend.

You stand still and stare.

What do you see?

Flashing yellow eyes in the alder tree, in the honeysuckle bush,
    cat's eyes which you hate?

Is a ghost approaching you, holding bloody tripe in flapping hands—
    and your long nose scents the prey?

Or are you just a dwelling for a strange, incomprehensible soul
    that sometimes leaves its animal abode an empty, transparent shell?

It wanders

Over meadows, among bronze-colored chrysanthemums and you await
        the return.

Is it getting near?

My hand touches the cool, smooth lizard brow . . . a collar jingles.

Obedient, my fair, mute companion trots beside me, homeward.

The poet Nelly Sachs, a contemporary who escaped Gertrud Kolmar's fate by a hair's breadth, dedicated her poem "The Visionary" to
G. C. (Gertrud Chodziesner):

You saw the thoughts circling
Like pictures around a head.
You believed in the air
Wherein the stars would rise again.

And you were not blinded
By time grown old.
Where for us was still evening
You already espied eternity.

My Gaze Is Turned Inward

LETTERS TO FAMILY MEMBERS
1938–1943

❖

I

Finkenkrug, September 13, 1938

Dear Hilde,

I didn't show your letter to anyone. I was deeply touched, not to say, shaken. You write: "for I love nothing better than my business and my work." I was not aware of that. . . . Don't misunderstand me. Of course, I was never that blind or insensitive not to see how devoted you were to your work. But I presumed this was due to your special talent for the book trade which was always superior to your husband's—were it the other way around, were he to prove the better in everything and your business would flourish without your contribution then, I always believed, your "love for the business" would also be less strong. . . . (It is quite possible that what I'm saying here does contain a kernel of truth.) I can imagine that such an "absolute" love for an occupation, a love that has nothing to do with husband or child, that such a love can exist; but I cannot empathize. This is not a value judgment. And if you believe yourself to be happier if you had a different, a less "masculine" attitude, then I must unfortunately confess that for many, many years of my life I would have been less unhappy had I had such a "masculine" attitude and had I not regarded my work merely as a sort of stopgap. I remember Ella used to chide me when I was working as a translator because despite my absolute love for what I was doing, I would have been ready immediately to throw in the towel if—But that is the way it goes, one lacks the wine and the other the goblet. And if you think that I did not "get stuck in the initial stages," then I might add that I paid a very, very high price for this completion. Today, I know, of course, that I was not cheated in the bargain, that what I received was worth the price—I wish you a similar fulfillment some day and hope that your child will help you to reach it. . . . I must admit that in years past, I used to live in outright terror whenever she would spend an extended period of time with us. Not because it meant more work, not at all, but because her mere existence reminded me so painfully and deeply of that which I did not have. . . . And yet, I was often also very happy to have the "little monster" stay with us. At times I miss her very much now and almost every day I quote some of the things she used to say so I can at least remember. You say a child is not a "personal achievement," but do only personal achievements reward us and make us feel happy? Somebody once said that the best gifts often fall into our lap undeserved. Be this as it may, my art too used to be something that "just happened." Certainly meanwhile I have contributed my share to the growth of the plant, but the seed was there first without being fostered by me.

Did you know, by the way, that the name of Emperor Hadrian's wife was also Sabine? I learned this only the other day while I was leafing through the Brockhaus.

I'd be glad to send you the two copies of my book you requested. But from your letter it is not quite clear whether you want me to enter the dedication into one of the volumes or whether you want one now for yourself and one later for Sabine. If it is to be for yourself, then I think it would be best if you picked the poem you like best and I'll dedicate it to you. If you would like the dedication to appear in the volume I already sent you, then maybe I can write it on a piece of gummed paper and you can paste it in. You need not write if you don't feel like it. Why not answer my question in a letter to Peter? He can let me know by postcard. At any rate, I won't send off the two volumes until I hear from you.

Vati would probably like to add something, but I don't want to show him this letter and so I greet you from myself only but from the heart,

Your sister,

TRUDE

P.S. Vati and I sent a card to the "monster" at the children's home. We hope it arrived.

2

Finkenkrug, September 18, 1938

Dear Hilde,

I expressed my good wishes to you already in my last letter. I could merely repeat them here. May you find in your life that, no matter how high the price you had to pay, it was worth the rewards you received in the exchange. And if you cannot find it today, then someday . . . I wrote you in detail about the books you asked for and maybe you'll let Peter know. After all I wouldn't want to write a dedication in a volume that you might want to pass along.

With very best regards for you and the "main character,"

TRUDE

3

October 16, 1938

Dear Hilde,

No, I'm not angry with you for not answering my letter sooner. And in turn, I'm sure you aren't angry with me if I write posthaste. Today is Sunday—and in the near future, I will hardly have time during the week to answer letters since I decided to learn to cook once again. Since last Monday, I'm taking lessons from "my" reader, who is a very good and experienced cook. Until recently she had been practicing her art also on a grand scale, that is, as cook for a school. She lives, convenient for me, in Eichkamp, and one of our table guests is a grass widower who has to eat whatever we prepare. I enjoy the lessons, and so does she, I believe. (Helene doesn't know anything about this, and it would be better if she didn't hear of it for the time being; she assumes that I'm busy somewhere with a desk job.)

I'm learning to cook the way you study English and Spanish, likewise without knowing whether I will ever be able to put this knowledge to good use. But aside from the fact that there's never any harm in having a skill of any kind, the mere sense of mastering something strengthens the heart. When I first began to study languages, I had no idea that one day this knowledge would be a trump card in my hand. If I'm now in a better psychological condition than those who are otherwise no worse off than I am, it is due to the fact that I can tell myself with confidence: "No matter where you may end up, you will be able to communicate immediately or within a short while." Of course, it is, as I said, not only this awareness that keeps me going. . . .

From what you write in your letter, I gather that you miss a few "encouraging" words from me. I would like to say them, but—I just can't. What I mean is that someone who is not in your situation cannot possibly feel what it is like and that any "consoling" words would be nothing more than "plain clichés." With all the words of encouragement I might give you, I would feel like someone who instead of giving a starving person a piece of bread gives him a pat on the shoulder with the remark: "Don't dismay, my good man, we have charitable people in our town. I'm sure you will get something from somewhere." Excuse this frankness—maybe not. I hope you'll find something suitable somewhere at your present place of residence.

I just wrapped two books (one with dedication) so "in-between." The package will be posted to you on Tuesday. Reviews have now appeared everywhere—often very prominent, generally heaping even more admiration and praise on *Woman and Animals* than the reviewer from the *C. V. [Central-Verein Zeitung]*. Due to the conspicuousness of our name, the reviews are being discussed in the widest circles, and I'm reminded of Byron's remark: "I awoke one morning and found myself famous." (Though it's not quite that bad in my case yet.) But even though I have been declared "the most important Jewish woman poet since Else Lasker-Schüler," it gives Vati more pleasure than me. I'm not very excited by it all. There once was a time when praise from strangers would have been welcome and would have been fruitful (only I rarely sought it and therefore mostly didn't get it). Today I know my worth as a poet without critics, what I'm able to do and what not. . . . I cannot empathize with Nero who sought the applause of the people in the arena. In his place I would have regarded poetry as a precious gift, reserved for a select few.

I have often read about Jean Giono but haven't read anything by him yet, though I often told myself that I would do it some day. Lately it has been getting more difficult to read novels, even good ones. Maybe it is because one now lives some to which the written ones cannot be compared. . . .

Sabine's ears must now be ringing all the time, since I'm quoting her at every fitting and unfitting occasion. But she has probably long outgrown these infantile expressions. And now that she is older and wiser—what beautiful stories I could tell her were she here.

A letter came from Lindenheims day before yesterday. They enjoyed your card. Vati too thanks you for the letter. He was especially pleased to hear that you are in contact with the relatives of Mrs. B. He hopes that this will turn out to your advantage.

Be well now and take this greeting from the heart of

TRUDE

4

November 24, 1938

Dear Hilde,

I'm no friend of saying "yes" today and "no" tomorrow, but I have to ask you to hold the "English" matter in abeyance for a while. I'm sorry you had to expend so much effort and money. But we are not masters of the course of events here. *Yesterday, we sold our house,* will probably have to move in about four to eight weeks. Helene wants to retire, and since the plans Vati had made in case I should be able to obtain a position as tutor in England must be filed away, I want to stay for the time being. I can and will not leave Vati alone at his age and under the present circumstances. You understand that, don't you? And you won't be angry with me? . . .

You'll hear more later (when we'll know more ourselves).

Give my regards, when you see her, to the dear child. With greetings from Vati and

TRUDE

5

Finkenkrug, December 23, 1938

Dear Hilde,

Many thanks for your letter and your great efforts on my behalf. I made several telephone calls about this matter already but will be able to pursue it more vigorously only after our move to Berlin. It requires a lot of footwork, which, in turn, requires a lot of time—and time is what I don't have right now. We have to be out of here between January 15 and 31, and we have to and want to "limit" ourselves and you can imagine—no, you can't imagine—what has accumulated in our house since 1923 or even since 1894. All this has to be unpacked, gathered, and sorted out, and most of it has to be given away (inasmuch as somebody can be found who wants it). I went to work right after the sale of the house, and I'm rummaging from morning till night and yet despair of ever getting done by mid-January.

But I'm not writing to give you an earful and to moan and groan—things are difficult enough for you too—rather I want to thank you for your good wishes for my birthday and return the same for yours. The very, very best for Püppi, who, I'm sure, will be with you for the Christmas holidays. Here the ground is covered thick with snow. I'm reminded of last year when I went sledding with the child. . . . I also remember when Vati showed her in the "Brehm" the giant butterflies and told her they were found in America, in Brazil, and she declared she wanted to go there and collect them when she was grown up. "When Püppi is big." Now she is big. . . . I never thanked you for the Giono. I'll do that as soon as I get around to reading it, which will hopefully be after our move.

For now many greetings from the heart

TRUDE

6

February 15, 1939

Dear Hilde,

Vati has been waiting for several days already for an addendum from me. But in the evening I'm always dead tired and during the day I have no time—so I just took it. For our move, which began in November, did not end for me with our settling in at Speyererstrasse. There is still so much that needs to be removed, stored, and eliminated. I don't know if you are aware that we were unable, despite all the "dumping," to get all our belongings into the three rooms we are going to occupy. The two front rooms we had originally planned to rent out unfurnished. So we had to furnish all five rooms and lease only the one in the back to a lady who doesn't pay anything but helps me with the housework. She is friendly and obliging but a total newcomer to physical work (which, in her case, even counts grinding coffee beans), and her interminable chatter and inability to be alone and a tendency to come to me every fifteen minutes with some kind of news, some request, some nonsense, all this makes any association with her a greater strain than all the housework. I would send her away and try to get along without her despite the overwhelming burden, but she is fifty-two, homeless, and without work. I feel sorry for her, and I will try to fortify myself against her talkativeness with friendly but obstinate silence. I did this already today, and I'm actually not as downbeat and tired as usual. . . .

By the way, what really gives me pleasure, and for which I wish I had more time, is cooking. I wonder if I have a hidden talent for it, or maybe the credit should go to my excellent teacher; enough, so far not only has nothing gone wrong that I have attempted, everything has turned out especially well. A few desserts of my own invention have earned Vati's applause. Perhaps cooking is also a form of poetry for an imaginative woman.

I'm just noticing that these lines are very prosaic, very "homely," but that is the way it has to be sometimes. I would have liked to talk more about you, also your last letter—for which I still owe you thanks—but I don't have it handy since I haven't unpacked my brown-painted strongbox, where it is safely preserved. But I do want to talk with you about the "England matter."

Every time I think about it, I feel bad about all the effort and cost you have expended for my sake, and that in addition to all your work that is piling up. The plan was this: I would see if I could get to England and then have Vati follow me somehow. In case I were to leave, he wanted to relinquish the apartment, sell some of our things, and store others in the attic, and move into a home. But the plans he had for himself are no longer possible—partly for external and partly for internal reasons—and so there's only one option for me in the nearest future, which includes him. We are in the process of taking certain steps, but this cannot be discussed yet. . . .

It may be that you didn't send me the addresses for nought after all.—I always feel that I have to apologize when I make unnecessary demands on you, although it's not my fault. But you aren't angry with me on that account, are you?

I really missed little Bienelein during the move. She would have been constantly underfoot, of course. But I often imagine with what pleasure she would have participated in all these highly interesting things. "Helping Opa, watching men." The packers, the movers, all the activities, putting things together, packing, and carrying, emptying the entire house, she would have eagerly taken part in all of this. Lugano is certainly objectively speaking more beautiful than a house move—but subjectively—for a child?

Maybe I'll get around to reading a little at least after supper soon. The first book I want to take up is the Giono. The packers put it fortunately in the library, so I won't have to search for it as for so many other things.

The Junge was here this morning and told Vati (I was not home and saw him only as he was leaving) that he had heard from you.

Now it's time for setting the supper table. Be well, say hello to the little monster—also to Peter if he is still there—and let me soon hear something encouraging about your prospects for the future.

Thinking of you a lot, and greeting you from the heart

YOUR SISTER TRUDE

7

Berlin, March 26, 1939

Dear Hilde,

Vati went to Stahnsdorf yesterday. I wanted to go today. But in the morning, the heavens poured out such an ugly snow shower that Vati wouldn't let me go. He said it was too wintry, everything is snowed in, and the garden shops at the cemetery didn't have any flowering potted plants yet. Yesterday the sun was shining at least. I hope to go on a nicer day during the week.

To begin right away with the ending of your letter:

I can understand that you are hungry for a new challenge. I also know how much satisfaction you gain from your accomplishments. But today I can see (it was not always that way) that the time of *preparation* for this challenge, this achievement, which is still completely in the dark, is of equal importance and value. The seed can only germinate if it grows for a while underground. Nobody told me that when I was younger. Maybe it is good that I tell you this today. Maybe the time of preparation has come for you now, even if you are yourself hardly aware of it. When I read your letters, I sometimes have a feeling I never had before when you spoke to me; it seems to me that you have embarked on a journey that I would like to call the "path toward the inner self." (Isn't there a book by Hermann Hesse of such a title or a similar one?) "Being prepared is everything." I believe that being prepared for the challenge is at least as important as the achievement itself, and the achievement is, in turn, more important than any success that may result from it. I don't just mean success in a negative sense but success in a positive sense. It may seem strange to you in the end for me to confess: the fact that my work means something to others, although quite welcome, does not give me as much joy as the act of creating itself. I feel about my little work the way a mother feels about a newborn child. Of course, she is pleased about the father's enthusiasm, the grandparents', the congratulations from relatives, but the main thing remains that the greatest joy comes from the fact that she brought the child into the world. That's why my favorite and best poems are the last two, because they are unpublished and have not yet found an echo. I mention this because I have a favor to ask of you. I would like to send you a copy of each of these two works ("Verszyklus" and "Drama"). I would like you to take them into custody, so to speak, since I don't know what fate has in store for me, where I might end up. Of course, I want you to read them if you like. Please let me know in your next letter if it is all right for me to mail them to you.

Yesterday afternoon I paid a visit to the poet Jakob Picard. He gave me an essay Bertha Badt-Strauss had written about me for *Der Morgen*. She sent it to him for me. The proofs were ready when *Der Morgen* had to cease publication. So the essay was already in print but unpublished. I thanked the author by telephone, and she expressed the wish to make my acquaintance. When this happens, I'll try to get a copy of the proofs for you. Otherwise, if you do want to read it, I will copy it for you when I have a chance. Father thinks the later the reviews, the better they are.

Now I'd better stop talking about myself all the time and make sure that I touched on all the topics in your letter.

Well, the problems with the tenants have not ebbed for me; however, I have now reached a stage (especially since it is presumably not a lasting condition) to regard matters from a humorous side. "Lotte, you old, fat, sentimental Warthe flounder" (she's originally from Landsberg) is how a nephew addressed her very poignantly in a letter. That she should be dissolving in tears today because good friends of hers are going to Kanga is understandable considering the way she is; I feel sorry for her; but her declaration that she will die of a broken heart aroused in me more laughter than sympathy. A fifty-two-year-old adolescent . . .

I hardly believe that it is your fault if you don't get along with Margot. Your description of her visit to Zurich only confirms my own experience. I could have told you very similar stories about her visits to Finkenkrug in past years. But why it all turned out that way, I'm unable to explain without a closer investigation; however, I'm little inclined toward such an investigation.

To turn to something more pleasant: I wonder what the little monster is up to now. Vati and I wrote her a longish letter to Montagnola. Who knows when and if I will see her again. But I'm content to think of her somewhere in this beautiful country, in the care of loving people, where she can play and she is happy. . . .

Vati sends his thanks for the letter he received from you yesterday. Mrs. Horwitz made a drawing of him this morning—for the second time. She's now frequently short of suitable models, and she asked him through me to sit for her.

Now I must close. I've been writing this letter, with interruptions, in the morning and afternoon. But I enjoy writing to you. Mutti surely wouldn't be angry with me for sending greetings to her youngest and favorite daughter instead of going to Stahnsdorf.

I remain,

YOUR SISTER TRUDE

8

Berlin, May 13, 1939

Dear Hilde,

A free afternoon today (which happens rarely) and the weather is nice for a change after a long cool, rainy period. So I had the "good idea" (as Bienelein would say) to sit on the balcony and finally start reading the *Träumer* you gave me. It didn't work. The noise from the street gave me the feeling of being right in the midst of it despite being two flights above it. And apparently, I still have not gotten used to the various automobile emissions in place of the fresh spring air. So I decided to withdraw into my quiet chamber and to thank you for the beautiful long letter and the "printed matter" that followed. The "Sechseläuten" reminded me of a poem by Gottfried Keller, the "Wegelied," which begins with the words "Three yards of good banner silk, a mass of honorable folk . . . ," even if it does not exactly sing about the same thing. It is a pity that our Püppi was not with us; it would have been such a pleasure to see her beaming little face. I would have liked to be there at any rate. . . . I try very hard to relate somehow to my local, landscapeless surroundings, but to no avail. Yesterday I walked along Martin Luther and then took Neue Winterfelder Strasse. These are streets I know as yet very little. Suddenly I noticed, somewhat baffled, that unlike my usual habit, I did not look at the houses, the shops, the people I met. "You must keep your eyes peeled, be vigilant," I commanded myself. Good. Five minutes later, again I stopped seeing, my gaze was turned inward again like a daydreaming, inattentive pupil in a classroom. It is now almost half a year since we moved here, and I find it simply impossible to develop any kind of relationship, either bear-able or unbearable, to these surroundings; I'm as much a stranger here as on the first day. Maybe this comes from the impersonal, sterile at-mosphere of this area; it might be different were we to live in another part of Berlin; but I might just simply not be able to get used to liv-ing in such a large city so far removed from nature. Even though I was born here. One cannot transplant old trees. . . . Hamburg. Another big city. But there in the center of town is the Alster River with its quays and seagulls.

But now of something different.

You are certainly right to say that most people who leave home are seeking a means of existence while you demand a calling; I hope that both will come together for you in the not all too distant future. As for myself, I am made of a very different mold and presumably would have dedicated myself to household and raising children without missing out on anything. And, believe me, without becoming superficial and shallow in the process. No, for me these simple, everyday things would have had a different, deeper meaning than they have for most women. My calling always rested quietly *in* me, and there it remains, and what I'm seeking is a suitable setting in which to dedicate myself to it. And I don't know . . . somehow I always thought that this suitable setting could not be found in America. I cannot get around the fact that my face is—as in our prayer—always turned toward the East and that this is not some "newfangled fad" with me, you know very well. It came early to the fore: it was not for nothing that my best friend was Hilda Josan at the age of nine. The Josans were very Asiatic Russians, had lived in Siberia and China. . . . I guess I'm myself an "Asiatic manqué" and would be glad if this hindrance could be removed. As a European it would probably be easier for me to set out for the West. . . .

That you should describe Püppi as an "accidental accomplish-ment": there I cannot agree with you. I don't quite believe in acciden-tal accomplishments in this "area." Should the "monster" one day, somehow, and by some means, become famous and stimulate some-body to write about her life, I'm certain that he would discover in you (and Peter) the gift of the select in miniature form, so to speak, or at least some seedling of the flower which is then blossoming in her. By the way, isn't her talent for dance not merely part of her mimetic abil-ity, which she no doubt has? I still remember when she played Shirley Temple for Vati, Helene, and me. . . . You say she resembles me in her movements. It would be funny if she showed a talent for dancing, which I too have to a certain degree and which might be strengthened through early training and be brought to maturity. That, by the way, is Mutti's legacy. . . . Sabine, in the picture—apparently indestructible—with the mule reminds me of Titania in *Midsummer-Night's Dream. . . .*

My "collected" works are still not unpacked since the move. It looks as if I will get around to pulling out what I want to send you in the next few weeks. Three items, I believe, two verse cycles and a drama. This move in winter and spring was not good for my Pegasus. But I'm sure it will pull itself up again . . . and will carry me on its back to a more beautiful land.

May 14.—I wanted to add a few more words last night, but after supper and washing the dishes, I was too lazy so I saved this little left-over for today. I nap for an hour or more after meals, but I also get up earlier than in Finkenkrug, about six or shortly thereafter. I try to be at Bolle shortly after opening at 7:00; whenever I get there at 7:30, the best rolls are all sold out, and then I have to go to the bakery. Even though this is close by as well; but it's convenient to get the entire breakfast, milk and baked goods, in one place and next door at that. Since I didn't get up before seven today, I feel like a late riser and feel beautifully rested. I'll be meeting Vati at a quarter to twelve—he's out taking his walk—in front of a little restaurant where we'll have lunch—so I don't have to cook—then I'll take a ride out to Weißensee (tomorrow is grandmother's birthday) and from there to L's on Baumschulweg, where I haven't been since we moved here.

This is all the current news. And now be well and try not to drive yourself too much. Until we write again.

YOUR BIG SISTER

9

Berlin, September 10, 1939

Dear Hilde,

Thank you for dropping the lines—even if this time they really were only lines. I certainly would like to read a report of your Greek journey ("Greek Travels" sounds already like the title of a book). I probably would have had to overcome more reticence than you before embarking on such a journey. Apart from the fact that I'm not much of a traveler, I would feel ever so lost in a country whose language I don't know. For somebody who has only little or no knowledge of foreign languages, it may not matter where he ends up abroad. But I, who felt not at all like a stranger in the old days in Dijon and Paris, would be afraid of my likely helplessness in Rome or Venice. (Although one can surely get by there with German, French, and English; but that would always be patchwork.) Among my "treasures," by the way, is a grubby little stone: a piece of marble from the Acropolis which Grandma Sch. [Schoenfliess] brought back for me from her Near Eastern travels which I kept since, carefully guarded, in my jewelry box. Now, you have seen the whole thing. . . .

I can picture the "monster" very well with braids tied in a ribbon (a red one?). I have been very "homesick" lately for her—called forth by the visit several days ago of her cousin. I tell him the same stories, recite the same verses as I did in the old days for her, and occasionally I even call him "monster"! I hope Sabine will forgive me for bestowing her title on somebody else; I feel myself that it is unfair. For even though Wolfgang displays one particular side of the monster; that is, he is just as difficult to handle (probably due to the lack of the stricter hand of the father), he still lacks a monster's special, magical qualities, which Sabine possessed. This comes alone from the fact that she had more of an inner stillness. He is a real boy, a sweet, lively fellow with a good eye and a sharp ear for everyday things, practical life, and a plethora of apt statements (as when he suddenly proclaims with a glance at my picture that Goethe could ride a motorcycle; that he was young enough—which he concludes from the fact that Goethe wears no hat despite his quite thinned hair and that he reads his letter without glasses). But Sabine is more imaginative; while his questions probe more the nature of concrete things, of that which is visible, she probes more the nature of the essence of things, of that which is invisible. I notice this repeatedly. . . . She once asked me, "What is a monster?"— he gets a kick out of the expression. (I don't forget that she was about four years old when I last saw her, while he is only four now.) He lives more "extensive"; she lived more intensive. I'm saying "lived" because I don't know how she developed since. It may seem strange, even ridiculous, that I make such observations about the individuality of three-year-olds "as if they were adults." But to a layman, all pearls are alike, though they are not exchangeable to the eye of the expert. This reminds me that Sabine's talent for dance may already have been indicated by the fact that she loved to hear me read to her in French, without understanding a word, just for the sake of the rhythm.

Justice Pakscher just called to inquire about Vati. He also asked about you and sends his regards.

Now summer is passing. We still had a few nice, warm days, and still I got very little out of them. Walks in the streets are not for me. . . . If this might continue for years . . . But the future is dark. And even if it were possible for me to get away from here soon (which is still within the realm of possibility), I could not take advantage of such an opportunity; for I cannot and will not leave Vati alone, especially now. He himself would not like to remain alone, since the Junge is now gone too. . . . and only paid help, probably hard to find anyway, to care for him . . .

Helene sends greetings; she is returning home after a three-month stay here.

Give the monster a kiss for me (how nicely I could tell her stories now!) Be very, very well, and write again to your sister,

TRUDE

10

October 1, 1939

Dear Hilde!

Finally! Finally a day when I don't have to "hop and shop," and when I'm not "hopping and shopping," straightening my room in great haste (and something always remains undone after all), and when I can thank you for your long letter and chat with you in leisure. Actually, I didn't have to call out "finally!" I just realize that your letter is dated September 14; this isn't all that long, but it seems to me as if many weeks had gone by. All days have been so filled with events. . . . world events . . . Not as if the events of the world grip me, engage me the way they did in the old days. It seems to me that things today change face and form with such rapidity; everything changes, even whirls, nothing stands still, and what used to change in the course of years or decades, now requires only days. And I, meanwhile, have withdrawn into the realm of the immutable, the existing, the eternal cycle of events (this eternal cycle of events need not be only "religion," it can also be called "nature" or "love"); seen from this vantage point, the events of the day appear to me as through a kaleidoscope: a figure has hardly been formed, when a shake, a turn, combines the colorful pieces of glass into a different formation, and it is almost impossible, useless, to try to remember the manifold forms and colors of the rays and stars. It may happen on occasion that something grabs my attention, as in the old days, that I discuss it and warm to it. But later I'm always somewhat amazed about myself, and I ask myself why I should have spoken in such a heated manner about things that hardly touch my inner being. I believe I wrote you once before about my sense of irreality where our life in Berlin is concerned; this too may be heightening my detachment. Meanwhile, this sense has become even stronger, even more like a spell; especially outdoors, in the street, I often have the feeling of being anesthetized, of being in a trance, from which I long in vain to wake up. Last Monday, when I had a little less to do, Vati took me— to "draw me out" a little—to an unfamiliar, remote part of the city park. I didn't let him see it, but this walk only made me hopelessly sad; I felt so old when I returned home. I know I often say "at home" when I speak about Finkenkrug. . . . "at home we used to do it this and that way." . . . as if the apartment in the Speyererstrasse was not "home" but "at other people's." I didn't even know as long as we lived in F. that I was so attached to it, and the thought of moving to Berlin didn't make me at all uneasy then. Maybe it is not F. I'm missing but more specifically that which is permanent, animal and plant, that which recurs eternally, that which is constant in its decaying and becoming. Somewhere in this neighborhood are several borzois. I cannot look at them without being painfully reminded of Flora, and yet I'm glad for her sake that she didn't accompany us. I stop in front of every newly discovered stationery store and look over the usually numerous dog picture postcards to see whether there is a Flora among them which I could send to Bienelein. But so far my search has not been successful. Last night, I thought again about the child. . . . about the winter before last when she came to us for a visit and how happy she was sledding with me in her warm wool suit. She probably can do this in Switzerland too, and even better, alas, without Aunt Trude, which is understandably more of a concern for Aunt Trude than for the child.

I'm enclosing one of several unretouched passport photos I had taken some time ago to be used as gifts and which I don't need. Most of them turned out awful (as such things almost always do); the enclosed one is just passable.

Margot's address is Dr. Margot (spell out first name) Chodziesner, c/o Australian Jewish Welfare Society, Sydney (N.S.W.), 146 Darlinghurst Road, Darlinghurst.

Vati is out taking a walk in the park with Peter. I'll wait with posting the letter until he returns. Write again soon when you're not too busy (you promised the travel report). With greetings from the heart to you and the monster,

TRUDE

11

Berlin, October 22, 1939

Dear Hilde,

I was just preparing breakfast when I found your letter in the hall. I put it, unopened, in my room since I didn't want to let Vati wait. Vati said later I should have opened it right away to see whether there was something urgent that needed a quick response. I replied that it wasn't your habit to write to me about such urgent things, only things that needed to be read in quiet. It gave me great pleasure to find that you wrote about my letters in the same tone in which I spoke to Vati about yours.

I'm glad that you like to read my letters. This acknowledgment encourages me to write. I'm generally not known to be an excellent letter writer, and it is true that I have little inclination for so-called natural letters which describe concrete things, the course of daily life. Margot, for instance, does this very well. I can do this only when I have experienced something really new, when I'm traveling in foreign surroundings. Otherwise, whenever I'm expected to write without con-

straint, I really have to strain myself. It's just not my nature to write
the way I speak. And should I not be able, for some reason, to correspond in the way that suits me, then the addressee won't be getting
anything that is beautiful or right. . . .

First to the unpleasant, or said more mildly, the less pleasant: the
information about Thea's state of health. I'm sorry that she wrote you
about it and in the process "bowled" you over. I'm sure she didn't anticipate the effect of her message. I saw from a letter from her parents,
which she showed me, that she had told them about her condition as
well; their way of dealing with it was a few consoling and hopeful
words. When I think of how our parents would have had a fit in such
a case—but we would have kept our illnesses from them if at all possible for that very reason and would have told them only in passing after we were well again. This as an explanation of Thea's account and
her excuses; she hardly thought that something that apparently left
little impression on her parents would "bowl" you over.

Now to the essential: Thea consulted Dr. Schwinke, a friend of Uncle
Siege, about her stomach ailment. He concluded that it was an ulcer
since she didn't respond to the diet he had prescribed, and he prepared
her for an operation. (You can well imagine how depressed she was—
maybe her letter was written at that time.) Of course, she then went to
a specialist, who for his part did not think it was an ulcer, advised again
a diet, and prescribed only tablets. Since she had been without pain for a
week and since an ulcer wouldn't have been suppressed by the tablets,
the doctor declared (what I, by the way, thought from the beginning)
that her ailment was a nervous condition brought on by the external
living conditions and that she would, in case these should change for
the better, immediately get better: maybe a ticket to Chile would be the
best medicine. Unfortunately, it is natural for Thea that her subjective
condition is worse than her objective one. She's easily dispirited,
deeply depressed, so that, for example, her view of people and circumstances becomes clouded and much that is by far not as murky to the
impartial observer appears to her as gray in gray. It's our fervent hope
that a journey for her and the boy will soon be realized. Then everything will be well and in good order.—I've been answering a short
question in rather great detail, but I thought it important since your
brief mention showed great disquiet and concern about this matter.

No, I don't think it unjustified (even if it may be also "abnormal") that you should be searching for a timeless dialogue, timeless books. One should not believe that all those who are preoccupied so exclusively with the events of the day are really totally absorbed with this preoccupation in their innermost being. For many, and especially those who are outwardly untouched, this represents a new experience—a boxing championship, a train accident, a new novel, a new fashion, all these have, according to taste, already in essence the same meaning. But even with regard to those who don't fit my assessment, rest assured that you are in good company with your deviating viewpoints: the German classic writers experienced, lived through, the French Revolution, Napoleon, and the Wars of Liberation (Goethe, if not Schiller)—and little enough of these events is reflected in their work. Contemporary events are a little like Impressionist paintings. Regarded from up close, they are no more than a jumble of lines, specks, and dots, which combine into a recognizable whole only when observed from a distance. Do you know C. F. Meyer's poem "Unter den Sternen" ["Under the Stars"]? It speaks about how the struggle under the sun, the dust of the arena, rivets the gaze to the ground and that only the obstacle of darkness that veils the path raises the gaze of the embattled warrior toward the stars. It ends with the words:

Die heiligen Gesetze werden sichtbar
Das Kampfgeschrei verstummt. Der Tag ist richtbar.

[The holy laws become visible; the battle cry falls silent; the day is ready to be judged.]

One may well say that today the *day* is not yet ready to be judged unless we should be able to take refuge under a foreign sky, a starry heaven, and observe it from that distant vantage point. Maybe your striving for timelessness is such an attempt.

You think I can hardly imagine your loneliness; you are wrong. When most people swim along in the general river, it is only natural that he who doesn't jump into the water is left behind, quite alone, on the riverbank. The isolation becomes all the greater, the more friends, acquaintances, and relatives the one left behind has. If he lives outwardly alone, then he can make believe that his inner loneliness is only a consequence of his external isolation, that friends would understand, would agree, if only he had any. However, someone who, in the midst of numerous friends, does not encounter a like-minded soul cannot allow himself such a fantasy, such a hope, and he will be much lonelier than the one who is without friends. Those, whom I call "the great solitary figures" were by no means always alone. They had followers, admirers, friends, servants, but they were isolated from them by an invisible wall. Did you, by any chance, read my Tiberius drama? He too was such a solitary figure. . . .

Now I must close; I have written away the entire Sunday morning. I have treated Pipkin in a somewhat stepmotherly way today—I'm probably a little her stepmother—but she'll be getting a letter next time all to herself. Lenchen really loved the note and the beautiful painting, and she promises to write soon. Your letter to me concludes with the words: "Be well, as much as possible, and write soon again such a beautiful letter, which was a true balm for me and still is"; I would like to close my own letter with the same words. And best regards to both of you,

TRUDE

When you write to the Junge give him my very best regards!

12

Berlin, October 31, 1939

My dear Monster,

Do you know what I would like? I would like to be Dr. Golden Hair (Dr. Golden Hair is a pretty fairy tale I would like to tell you sometime if you were here). But why would I like to be Dr. Golden Hair now? I shall tell you. Because there is a little old man who visits Dr. Golden Hair and who takes a piece of soap from his pocket, pours water over it, makes foam, submerges a pipe in the foamy soap, blows into it, and makes a soap bubble. But this is not an ordinary one; it is a magic soap bubble. It grows and grows and becomes so big that Golden Hair, who is a pretty little boy, and the little old man can get inside. Then the soap bubble lifts off the ground slowly with the two inside and up into the air. They fly far, far away into a distant land. Something like this, like Golden Hair, I wish I could do too. But instead of the little old man, I would take on my trip my big, beautiful doll Elizabeth with whom I played when I was a child, the one with brown curls, blue eyes, and a pink dress. Can you guess for whom I would bring her along? (By the way, I gave the doll to your Papa for safekeeping for you.) Well, and then I would sit down in the soap bubble as in a gigantic glass sphere, and I would float above mountains, valleys, and rivers, above towns and villages; they all would be far, far below me and would look all tiny like the colorful wooden houses from a play box. And farther and farther away would I fly, above fields and forests until I would finally come to a very high mountain range, and my soap bubble would have to rise higher so it would not collide and burst. And what is this high mountain range? I believe it is the Alps, Switzerland. And suddenly below me appears a big city between the mountains. Do you know what this city is called? And then I press a little against the floor of the sphere, and the sphere begins to sink, lower and lower, until it passes the rooftops and glides down into the street and lands softly on the ground. And as I'm floating down, my eye just catches a sign saying "Landoltstrasse." The next moment there is a soft, cracking sound, and the bubble bursts and disappears completely, not even shards remain, only a bit of wet, glistening foam on the pavement. But I don't pay any attention to it; with my doll in my arms, I turn toward the house in front of which I set down, and I ring the doorbell. I didn't really have to ring, for an already pretty big girl (that is, completely grown she is not yet) happens to open the door just then.

"Oh," I ask, "is this the residence of Hilde Wenzel and Sabine Wenzel?"

"But I'm Sabine Wenzel myself," the girl explains.

"I know Sabine Wenzel from Grolmannstrasse very well; but she is a little child, not such a big girl."

"But I'm she."

"Impossible! Two years ago Sabine Wenzel was still a little worm, and you are almost a school girl. . . . I'm Sabine's aunt, that is, I never called her Sabine, but always "Monster" or "Püppi.""

"What!" the big girl calls out, "then you are my Aunt Trude. I didn't recognize you at all."

"I didn't recognize you either."

When the strange girl calls me Aunt Trude, then I know that it is really Sabine. But how should I have recognized her; she is almost as tall as I am. And since we spoke with such loud and lively voices, your Mutti peaks through the door to see what is happening.

"Oh, my God," she calls out. "It's Trude! And just today on Sabine's birthday. That is just too wonderful!"

And now I wish the monster a happy birthday and I give her the big doll and then we celebrate her birthday with coffee and cake. . . .

See, I made up this story. This is what I would like to do, even if it is not exactly your birthday. Then the three of us would be happy to see each other again and we would have a party. But, unfortunately, I cannot fly to you, because I don't have a magic soap bubble, nor am I Golden Hair, but simply

YOUR AUNT TRUDE

[about November 6, 1939]

My dear, little Monster!

Here is a card from Aunt Trude which had been given to her by a very old grandma when she was a little girl; Aunt Trude liked it so much then so she kept it until today and hopes that you will like it too. This is a parasol, not an umbrella, and I wish you lots of sunshine for your birthday and many nice presents. From me you will get a funny book which your Papa will send you and with which you can create many monsters as by magic—your Mutti will show you how to do that. Wolfgang got such a book for his birthday, and I thought you should have one too.

Give my regards to your Mutti. With greetings and kisses from your

AUNT TRUDE

13

Berlin, December 13, 1939

Dear Hilde,

Receiving your letter was enough to make me happy. It was the only one I received and promptly—two postcards arrived later, but that was all for this time. That you weren't in the right frame of mind while you were writing, I can well imagine. Today, I'll take my revenge, for I feel the same way. I feel somewhat tired and weak in the head from all the housework, and I would rather wait until Sunday morning, but the letter must be posted so it will arrive on time. First of all, let me wish you a happy birthday; maybe after that, things will get better.

So we didn't really celebrate this time. Vati's present, since I had no special wish, consisted of some money and a very beautiful carmine red alpine violet which is still blooming—(unfortunately, always only a brief pleasure!). I wasn't at all in the right frame of mind for a celebration. I know very well that I shouldn't permit myself to become overwhelmed by the darkness all around, that I should light the "inner light." But this knowledge is often of little help—when I absolutely cannot find the light to kindle. In the summer, there was still the shimmering of some beautiful trees along the way, a goldenrod, a lilac bush in front of the house, that lasted at least for a short while; of course, it made me see Finkenkrug as a lost paradise. . . . with all the birch trees, the beach tree, the forest . . . And with Flora . . . I think I already wrote to you that I didn't know before our move how attached I was to all that. But this "Bavarian" neighborhood is ghastly in winter. Even if no ghastlier than the Tauentzienstrasse or Nollendorf Platz. Yes, I was sometimes glad to see my dentist in Wedding; even though there is even less green there, but that part of town has at least character! Then again, would I want to live there? . . . At times I just feel like taking my coat and hat and wandering far, far away. More and more often, I now think of going out to Finkenkrug with the first snowfall where I could stomp around in the woods in the moonlight as I used to do. But I also know that I will never carry out this plan.—Tell me, what am I "moaning and groaning" like this in your ear (and on your birthday of which I have so far barely taken notice)? I'm not usually like this. . . . But it may be that this year of living in Berlin has given me a sensitive skin, which immediately feels every bit of pressure, whereas in the old days, I would have felt nothing more than a light strafing. It's been that way for some time now. . . . I remember in late summer I met a five-year-old girl holding a darling, still very young Skye terrier on a leash. When they had passed me and I turned around, I saw that the child had been starting to race without regard for the little animal, who could not keep up, and so she choked and pulled it. If the little girl hadn't been accompanied by an adult, I would have followed her and would have stopped her. The whole incident lasted probably no longer than a few minutes, but later I felt so pained in the heart as if I had witnessed something really very, very sad. . . .

And this is supposed to be a birthday letter? (I already made a mistake with writing "now" and almost wrote "no.") Please don't be angry with me. . . . For out of the abundance of the heart the mouth speaks. I'm still thinking about what you wrote about your health, that in your case it would be just the reverse of the way it is with Thea. . . . even if it were better than with Thea, I'm not happy about it, and if my best wishes are able to contribute something in this regard . . .

So far we received a postcard from Thea from Genoa, written on the day of her departure (I'm sure you heard from her meanwhile also).

Püppi, thank you for the beautiful bookmark and the wonderful handwritten card of the tenth. (What is it that you did and don't want to tell me?) It appears to us from the picture that she's grown a lot and is not as chubby as before; as always, she's laughing, looks a lot like Peter. By the way, what is it that she holds so lovingly against her little face, a piece of fur or a living or dead animal? The fairy tale of the angel (pardon me, the true story) is very nice, and we like especially the ending, the explanation how she "learned" it.

In this connection, it may please you to learn that the stand-up card which I inserted in Vati's picture book for Sabine is from Grandma Schoenfliess, which she once sent to her little granddaughter. I don't know if such cards still exist (the taste is debatable).—

Be very, very well in your new year of life; this I wish for you and also that you will celebrate the day more fittingly than I did mine. I think Püppi will make sure of that.

Always your

TRUDE

December 16
Postscript

Dear Hilde,

Had I written this whole letter today and now—it's seven o'clock in the morning—my tone would have been lighter. I spoke about the "inner light" and asked: "But what if there is no light to kindle?" And strangely, the next morning, a late birthday package arrived from Suse containing, beside delicious edibles, a tallow wax light. I like the fragrance of these lights very much—it reminds me of summer and flowers and bees. But in addition, somebody seemed to answer my question saying: "Here is the light you were looking for." And now it's a little brighter. . . . [. . .]

What else did I want to report? Oh, yes, that's it. Lindenheims have to move on January 3 and have rented an unfurnished room in this area: Berlin W., Regensburgerstrasse 27. Carriage house, c/o Ullmann.

Again best wishes,

TRUDE

14

Thursday, December 22, 1939

Dear Hilde,

This note is only to acknowledge receipt of your beautiful, long letter; more detailed thanks later—that I'm enjoying the "Greek Travels" very much, you can well imagine. Peter has also received two cards from you. Furthermore, I can tell you that Vati and I—especially Vati—sent a "really big" birthday letter to your address in Zurich—this message in case that you are already in Basel when it arrives. I believe I mailed it on the sixteenth of this month, and a few days later, Vati also sent, as you suggested, airmail letters to the children. They will probably arrive while you are in Basel.

Vati asked me to let you know that Aunt Emma died on the fifteenth of this month; she was seventy-two years old.

If nothing comes in between, Peter will visit us on your birthday for coffee, and if I have a chance, I will one of these days take up the "Greek Travels" again. I feel I must read it several times to derive the full pleasure. Thank you and also Sabine for her "dear Aunt Trude" who wishes you, also in the name of Vati, beautiful days of quiet joy.

[December 26, 1939]

[To Hilde, beginning is missing.] like a fairy tale, not to "experience" in the literal sense.

And then: I have been feeling for a long time here as if I was living in a strange land. And even if I migrated to a far-off region and be it the most beautiful, in my heart I would always remain "a wanderer, at home in two strange lands but without a true homeland." I long to return home. To a land further south and east of Hellas . . . For ever . . .

The pictures are sharp enough and it is probably due to my short-sightedness that I can recognize them clearly even without Vati's magnifying glass. Vati just passed through the room and sends greetings and best wishes for the New Year—until he'll be writing to you himself.—

Lately I've been reading again the Giono which you gave me for my birthday last year. That is, not from cover to cover, but here and there, pulling out passages I enjoyed. For you are right, it's not really a novel. It also has something very lively—varied and strong, lacking in unity, splendid and then again artless, at times terribly banal—like life.

But now I must close; it's almost nine and Vati has to get his sandwich. This is actually not a "real letter" just off the top of my head; but you won't take it the wrong way.

Your sister

TRUDE

15

Berlin, January 15, 1940

Dear Hilde,

Now I forgot, "in the heat of battle," in my reply to your card to thank Püppi for the beautifully written New Year's greetings with the "high mountain." The chocolate is already consumed—it was really outstanding, marvelous, brilliant, fabulous, fantastic, and whatever other new hyperboles there may be. I myself can't bear them—I don't mean the chocolate but the hyperboles—to my mind it's too dumb, for example, that a cup of coffee should be "brilliant," a sour herring "fantastic," and the Venus de Milo should be "outstanding." And one hears things of this sort.

Apropos matters linguistic. I'm not surprised that you are taken aback by the Junge's letters in the strictest sense. Actually, this cannot be otherwise. For example, when I had occasion to write a letter in French, I was often surprised on reading it over by the fluidity, lightness, even elegance of my writing style, more than I had expected of myself. And the more accomplished my writing turned out, the stranger I became to myself. So if my own writing in a foreign language appeared so strange, it is hardly surprising that the Junge's letters should contain little of his own personality. There is much more of essence one could say about this subject, but let this be enough. I don't want to write a treatise on linguistics. Ilse Benario reproached me many years ago (I believe I mentioned this before) for not writing letters but treatises, essays.

Speaking of Ilse: She sent us a few days ago a love package with all the good things the Dutch have at their disposal. It had been posted at three in the afternoon and was, according to the ticket, inspected at the local customs office by evening. Prompt service, at any rate.

To move from the corporeal back to the spiritual: You suggest that "perhaps we should, some time . . . write something together, in the tradition of several great models." You see, such a collaborative effort is something I was never able to understand. Among lesser talents, I might see the point; but I simply cannot imagine how the brothers Goncourt, for example, managed to work on their novels together. If I were asked to produce a poem in collaboration with another person, it would be as if two women shared in delivering a child. It just doesn't work. Each poetic creation is for me an act of giving birth (the labor pains are sometimes ghastly). At this moment, this event takes place in stages—always at night. I go to bed early, and when the tenants upstairs wake me with their rather noisy nightly return home, between one and three o'clock, then I have already had a few hours of sleep and the head work can begin. By the time I have "advanced" the "child" a few centimeters, it is already five o'clock, and I can go and doze a little more. In the morning, after I'm dressed, it gets written down right away. In the process, I get very tired, I feel miserable, and often have headaches. In short, all symptoms of a "hangover" as after a wild night of dissipation, which it actually was! The following night, I sleep off the effects of intoxication, and even the noisy tenants above cannot wake me—on the third night, the whole thing continues anew. I've tried on occasion to work during the day, the way I did in Finkenkrug, but first, I never have the necessary inner balance, and I'm always plagued with a bad conscience that I may be neglecting some chore around the house that needs doing. And second, without fail, Vati comes in to ask a favor or just to tell a story, and then I lose my thread and nothing comes of the spinning. You see, the fact that I'm letting you in on some "secrets of the trade" shows that I regard you already a little as a member of the "guild," of the "profession."

Concerning what you write about the émigrés and their illusions of a "new life," a "new homeland," I just want to say that I divide people into wild plants, potted plants, and cut flowers. Wild plants, if they are no longer young but still grow slightly, can blossom only with difficulty in foreign air. For potted plants, the most important thing is the pot; if they can retain it, that is, the familiar furniture, cooking facilities, favorite dishes, then they will feel good—air and country do not play much of a role for them. Cut flowers can be placed anywhere as long as a vessel with water is available. The vessel of water in that case is always a "job." The German terms—work, position, professional activity—don't quite fit. I don't want to speak about the difficulty of supplanting the wildflowers; but potted flowers will wither when the pot has been taken away and how many cut flowers for lack of water.

I was sorry to hear that you are frequently ill or never really quite well. But mere expressions of sympathy don't make it better, and since all I can do from here for you is write letters which you enjoy, I want to try at least that medicine. I have neglected Sabine today; she won't "sit on the sofa and sulk" because of it. I can't imagine that she should be turning into quite such a savage as you claim. The right mixture of love and strictness should remedy the situation. More about this some other time. Today warmest greetings to both of you,

TRUDE

16

January 28, 1940

My dear Monster,

Your Mutti has received enough letters from me for now. I think it's your turn again to get one. I'm thinking back about how much you liked sledding when you were in Finkenkrug—even though we haven't had a real snow winter in the last few years. Now, in Switzerland, it's probably much nicer for you. When I was seventeen, I once went sledding in the Mulde Mountains. It took about a quarter of an hour to pull the sled to the top of the mountain and five minutes to get back down to the bottom. I was staying at an estate then with many other young girls. We learned to cook, bake, sew, launder, and iron. But the best part about it in the wintertime were the sleigh rides. We had four or five really big, horse-drawn sleds with little bells and colorful pom-poms attached to the harness. When the sleds drove across the field one after the other, the bells made a pretty, tingling sound. The coachmen strangely did not sit on the box but behind us on a small, elevated seat without a back and held the reins above our heads. Your Mutti might still remember this type of sled. She might even remember the big red box sled your Aunt Margot and I had when we were children. It was more a coach than a sled for two seated opposite each other. It had to be pushed from behind by an adult since it was much too heavy for a child. A toboggan would have been much more practical for us. But they didn't exist then for children to play in, only for sport. At any rate, one day Aunt Margot and I decided to slide down a winding path in this monstrous contraption. We got in and rocked until the thing started to move and began to slide slowly downward. But since we had no way of steering, it landed gently against a tree— and turned on its side. The type of toboggan children have now would have tipped over and gone to pieces. Our sled was much too heavy and solid. It merely sustained a small crack in the side and somewhere a little piece of wood was chipped off—that was all. And the two of us were unharmed. Your Mutti once flipped over in a different way while she was sledding. . . . Our school was quite a long distance from home, and we always took the tram. When a lot of snow had fallen during the night and the streets had not yet been ploughed and the trains wouldn't run, then we had to walk. On such occasions we were, of course, late for school and usually with wet boots. The boots had to be taken off and laid out in front of the heater to dry. And all the girls sat in class in stockings. So this turned out to be only a "snow-and-sled" letter. But what can one write about in the wintertime?

With best regards, also for your Mutti,

YOUR AUNT TRUDE

17

January 28, 1940

Dear Junge,

It seems I'm thinking as much about Thea and the boy as Vati. Even more about the boy than about Thea since in the last few weeks [of their stay here], while Thea was running errands, he had frequently been entrusted to me. I own a movable, Japanese paper doll which Hilde bought some years ago at the Christmas mart; it turns, and you can turn with it, all kinds of tricks. [. . .] This trickster replaced a whole bag full of toys; it amused us for hours, and Vati says that he never heard Wolfgang laugh as much as with this game. Who is playing with him now? Every morning when I hear the rattling of the mail slot, I go to the door full of expectation, in the hope of finding a letter, but so far, nothing. . . .

As Vati said already, there is nothing new to report about us. I find it doubly difficult to be cooped up in a city apartment; more and more often, I yearn to take a ride out into the open country, to our "former area," to walk in the woods and stomp around in the thick snow; but when I remember that I will have to return to the city, I prefer to let it be. . . . Besides that, I still have a lot of work to do in the house and wouldn't be able to indulge in "personal pleasures" before it gets dark anyway.

For your birthday, I wish you all that you wish for yourself, everything you wished for Thea on her last birthday. [Ending is missing.]

18

January 29, 1940

Dear Hilde,

I don't know when I will be able to finish this letter and post it. But I would like to relate a little experience before it seems stale and flat to me. I want to capture my impression "red-handed" so to speak.

Yesterday, Sunday, I followed an invitation for tea with some friends who had moved from here to the Reichsstrasse last autumn. Since we had beautiful snow weather, I decided to start out right after lunch so I would have time for a walk around. [. . .] My path led me, of course, first along Ahornallee. I soon gained the impression of certain changes in the layout of the street. This was reinforced and confirmed in the course of my stroll. The changes were due, in part, to expansion and "modernization" of individual houses (to the point where they were unrecognizable sometimes) but even more to the fact that the owners of larger garden areas had parceled off their land into two or three lots and had sold them for construction of other houses. Consequently, there was a pattern of new houses inserted between two old, familiar houses. Sievert Park behind the Roethes' house (who are still living there) is thus filled with new construction. The same is true for the Rüttgers' expansive lot beyond Gottfried-Keller Strasse as well as the Marzahns' garden on Ulmenallee corner of Lindenplatz. In what used to be the "little woods" behind—or in front of—the Warnholtz Villa (which is unchanged and is now home of a publishing house), there are two new country-style homes, so close together that a third one could fit at the corner of Klaus-Groth Strasse. I had already seen the Gause-Wagner Villa in its remodeled state, but it is no longer our neighbor. On our former "new plot," a new building has risen, quite close to the street, which presses on our old house farther to the rear and makes it appear much smaller.

Our house . . . It looks older, shabbier, somewhat neglected and gray, but otherwise unchanged. Even the thermometer outside the living-room window is still there. The fence, which wasn't the youngest then, has become even more wobbly and completely rusty. The bell is missing from under the old bell roof. The door was wide open and a sign read: Police Station. I hesitated for a moment, then I entered.

I entered the garden in the rear of the house and stomped through the snow. There, too, no changes. From the lattice of the veranda, next to the stairs, a bird feeder was suspended. Inside the garden, I first had to find my way around. At first I didn't recognize the trees. Right in front of me on the lawn was the middle group of trees where the deer used to be and the snow-covered strange object nearby was our "pool." From my vantage point behind the house, I believe all this to be much farther away. It is possible that my memory had enlarged the garden. It is also possible that it seems smaller because of the subdivision of the plot and the new construction and also because across the street is a gigantic high-rise block along the extension of Soorstrasse, peeking through the old, black lattice fence. In addition, the unswept snow cover made everything seem the same and no piece of grass, no flowerbeds or pathways were distinguishable. All in all, the garden seems to have remained the same, though the gazebo is gone, nor is there a pavilion anymore on the hill. The vine espalier is still there and so is the acacia tree in front of the smoking room. Without having met anybody, I returned to the front door. But then I remembered that a police station was open to the public, and I decided to venture inside. . . . At the very worst, somebody would show me the door. So I mounted the front stairs and passed through the small vestibule into our "entrée" with the bench and mirror. Here I was met immediately by an officer who inquired about my purpose. I told him and wanted to leave right away. He asked about my name, and the caretaker, who was also present, he knew the name from old real estate deeds that were still being kept. I was asked to come in. The officer guided me through the corridor to the kitchen. In a word, everything seemed physically unchanged, only that everything was bright and freshly painted, clean and new in appearance. Only the back staircase to the gardener's quarter had been removed, as the officer told me; the door in the back corridor under the staircase is still there. I had already noticed that the wooden door to the garden had been replaced with a heavy iron door. I did not go all the way to the top floor (there hardly would have been anything to see anyway). Instead I glanced sideways into the living and smoking rooms and the salon. All these rooms are used as offices— no more wallpaper but brightly painted walls. The caretaker said he was Matischok's successor and has been in this position already ten years. I asked him whether the plans to cut a street through the prop-

erty had been given up. He said on the contrary, construction will begin soon. A sewer system had already been installed, and the neighbor
to the right (formerly Koeppens) had to give up a parcel of his garden.
I thanked him and left, returning to the Reichsstrasse via Ahorn-
Ulmen-Lindenallee.

This is all for now. I had been distracted from my little experience
shortly afterward. But now I wonder about myself that besides a certain inner interest, I was not more deeply touched. For some people,
such a visit would have been something of a "pilgrimage," a "return to
a lost paradise." For me, this was not so, perhaps because there was no
cloudless, blue sky above my childhood. In part, also for another reason. If one finds the home of one's parents inhabited by strangers—
different furniture, different people—then the comparison between
now and then may inspire some nostalgia. But there was actually little
to compare between these offices and our rooms; they were something
incomparable, something new, and left the memory of what once was
our habitat untouched. My imagination was quite capable of restor-
ing, without much ado, our old furniture to these bare, sober spaces;
had it been a private home, furnished in a homey way, it would have
been more difficult. Then I would have had to take the image of the
new chairs, tables, beds, lamps, curtains, and their arrangement and
would have had to watch out, in my mind, that the new furnishings
didn't displace ours. Helene looked up Matischoks once when she was
visiting Wally at the Paulinenhaus during her illness. She saw the
rooms then and spoke with enthusiasm about the chandelier and the
beautiful wallpaper the baron had put in. I wouldn't have liked it all
that much. . . .

Maybe you could pass on my description or at least its contents—
without subsequent remarks—to the Junge and Margot. I'm sure they
would read it with great interest. And who knows maybe even the
"monster" could understand it if it were explained right. More some
other time.

D. February 3, 1940

Yesterday, two pleasant surprises: (1) the letter from the Junge, and
(2) an airmail letter from Thea, mailed by Betty, who wrote that she
received in the same envelope a letter for Thea's parents and Georg,

which she posted right away. The letter indicated that Thea had already written a regular letter from Chile, which is probably on the way. This one is dated January 18. We learned from it that the immigrants were divided into various large groups and were assigned to several provincial towns. Thea had been quartered up to now in the best hotel in the city, but, as she writes, she just rented a room in a house whose owners are spending three months on their "fundo." Two other rooms in this house are occupied by a childless couple, the lawyer Schneider from Charlottenburg (who studied with Uncle Mole) and his wife; so the two renters seem to have the whole house to themselves, and a garden is there also. Thea will be sharing the chores around the house with the woman, who is very nice, so that there's always somebody to keep an eye on the boy when she is running errands. By the way, he seems to make friends everywhere among children and adults, who are eager to entertain him and take him on walks. He grew a lot and thinks that Pappi wouldn't recognize him because he's so big, neither would he recognize Mutti because she had become prettier. And, he wanted to know whether Mutti had brought shaving cream from Berlin since he would soon have to shave. . . .

Thea is in good health, therefore probably her improved appearance; her stomach is all right, which doesn't surprise me. The dark point in the otherwise bright picture is the question of employment; so far she has not been able to find a job but hopes confidently to find one, all the more since she heard that several passengers from the *Augustus* had been placed in smaller towns. It seems that there is less of an effort in Concepción to find placements; but she thinks it'll all work out. . . . The cost of living is apparently low; the room costs sixty pesos a month = two dollars.—Thea didn't see her friend during her brief stop in Santiago; but she wrote her a nice letter. Thea's address is now: Concepción, en lista de correos (general delivery). She apparently has not yet received the airmail letter we sent to Concepción on January 2 or 3 but did receive one sent earlier to the address of her friend.—I'm sure that you receive meanwhile the double letter for you and the Junge.

With greetings from

VATI AND TRUDE

February 22, 1940

Dear Hilde,

The "sky blue" little box (it seems like the blue of an Italian sky) arrived here yesterday morning and was welcomed with great anticipation and came under "attack" right away. The joy is only dampened by the thought, especially Vati feels that way about your packages, that you had to deny yourself this and that to make us such a present. This did not keep him from savoring the gustatory delight of your "kind gift," which I generously left to him alone. Many, many thanks from the bottom of my heart!

In front of me is your postcard from the seventh of this month where you write that you read my report from the Westend with "mixed emotions." You see, I wrote down this report immediately, "fresh from the barrel," without much pondering (inasmuch as it is possible not to ponder) but with the intent and the hope that it may please you. Now, I understand completely that your attitude toward what I related is, and must be, different from mine and that especially the tone of my narration should have been different. It is a truism: we cannot put ourselves in the place of even those who are closest to us; we cannot change ourselves totally. It happens less often, for example, that one says something malicious with the intent of stinging the other but it runs off his skin like water. More frequently, words spoken without the intent to harm will irritate and hurt the other. I once found in an art calendar of 1917 a little poem, which I don't remember, except for the last two lines, by a contemporary poet, whose name I don't remember:

This is the greatest comfort and greatest truth, to know that
I'm I and you are you.

I probably retained these lines because they expressed what seems so very true to me. "My love, my child, how wonderful/That we don't understand each other" runs an ironic verse by Max Brod. People nowadays, or I should say momentarily, people understand each other very little without this being very wonderful. Their sorrow, mostly real but sometimes merely imagined, has fostered in them a kind of emotional egotism that causes them, as soon as they are in the company of others, to blabber about their plight or their various experiences or the plight and experiences of their relatives and friends—and the partner in these exchanges then does perhaps the same, waiting only until Mr. X is finished with the report about his son in Rio in order to confirm, to add to, or to dispute what he has heard by relating the fate of a niece who also lives in Rio and then continues to talk for hours about his daughter in Buenos Aires. Sometimes I have the impression they are suffering from a "weak bladder"—these people simply cannot retain their affairs by themselves. Excuse the not very pretty expression, but I think it is apt. Maybe it is hard-hearted on my part to berate people for trying to alleviate the burden for each other by sharing their stories. . . . If that were only so, but it is not. They all go their own way, bent by their own yoke that they are hardly able to see that of the other and certainly don't think of lightening it for him—two are speaking, and none listens. I confess that I too frequently "howl with the wolves," simply because it is useless to sound a different tone. Afterward, I always feel quite depressed, and I'm glad to be alone again. In Finkenkrug there still was a definite, wholesome distance; but here, people are "clucking" close together. A few people are close to me—we form a quartet, two women and two men—when we get together, family and private affairs disappear somehow in the course of the conversation. But when one of the men brings his wife along, which happens occasionally (I don't like her very much), then these affairs resurface even if only temporarily.

Maybe I'm behaving like the people I'm scolding by expressing my opinion in such a blunt manner, and what I say in the heat of the argument might displease the listener. But from some of the things you say in your letters, I surmise that my view is not totally alien to you. . . .—As for the picture of the house—I never knew anything about the pictures of the grandparents—I didn't forget it. I had several in my "private" possession and wanted to donate one to you but couldn't find them despite a long search. Vati's pack is also buried forever. Sometime when Helene is here, I'll try to find one of the two green albums, which presumably contain pictures of the house and the grandparents, and take them out for you.—Strange. At this very moment, as I'm writing to you that the pictures are nowhere to be found, at this moment I know, as through a sudden revelation, where they are. Only I have to take the time sometime to dig them out. . . .

For now, be well. You see, I unburdened my heart to you; please do the same in return—believe me, I don't want to just talk by myself, but I will listen attentively and with great sympathy. Some of the remarks in your postcard seem to indicate that you could use a sympathetic ear. . . .

Now I must go to bed and before falling asleep I want to read— how many times has it been!—a little more in the *Buddenbrooks*. This book is in its way a classic work—solid and warm and as indestructible as Christian Buddenbrooks's suits.

Give my regards to the monster (I would tell her today a fairy tale about a child that fell asleep in the evening and woke up as a snowman the next morning—hopefully this is not almost close to the truth).

With very best regards,

TRUDE

The double letter from Chile arrived.

20

March 9, 1940

Dear Hilde,

Yes, your two "Easter eggs" arrived here in good condition. We haven't tasted the butter yet; the cheese tastes "fabulous" (really fabulous), and with regard to the cocoa, I dipped a little deeper into my modest supply of this product and served up a warm chocolate semolina porridge yesterday afternoon. I'm sure Helene will view the cold leftovers with a distrustful eye [. . .], but these days the motto is "Cook with Fantasy," and that is what I'm doing. I can and must report that even Helene seeks my advice sometimes, that she even thought my lemon flummery, which she at first instinctively rejected, was excellent, once she tasted it. She even declared that she wanted to make one herself at home. Naturally, I enjoy such triumphs silently. . . . Again, many thanks from the heart for your package.

Peter was here the evening before last and "absconded" with your letter after we had copied down the new address. I'm very happy for you and Sabine about the news. I can well empathize with your joyous anticipation of the move to new quarters—even though we have here a nice, warm apartment that is our own! But if I only once didn't have to look out of the window into the yard . . . I find myself much more dependent on the wider environment than the immediate space. It is not so much the view on the yard that is so unappealing; it is the whole area. . . . Just as the position I had in Hamburg in 1927 was so unpleasant and yet I hardly suffered from it because I liked the city so much. It was just the reverse in Peine. I don't know if you felt the same way. . . . possibly . . . Your apartment on Grolmannstrasse was certainly nothing to be envious about, and yet, I can imagine that you liked it because the business, your work, gave you pleasure. . . . (Am I right? After all, one cannot see the inside of even those who are closest to us.) When Helene would say that Finkenkrug was nicer than Grolmannstrasse, Sabine would always insist that Grolmannstrasse was very nice. . . . Does she still talk about the bookstore, or do the more recent experiences bury the past? It must be a great relief for you that she can play outside with her little friends without having to be supervised. For you, best wishes that you may "survive" the move. But with the gaze fixed on the "golden aim," I'm sure you will overcome all obstacles that are still in your way.

Best wishes for both of you!

TRUDE

21

Berlin, May 15, 1940

Dear Hilde,

You see, I wouldn't leave a beautiful, big letter such as yours of April 29 unanswered for long. You gave such a colorful description of your view from the window that I was able to picture it exactly. "Sometimes beauty hurts." I can understand that. . . . The beauty of this landscape is probably particularly strong, overwhelming, in the end, maybe even depressive, but it may be that the individual in his rest-less, uncertain, fleeting existence stands in contrast to water, earth, and sky in their immutable, quiet permanence, despite all transformation that touches the heart. . . . "This is how you are, and this is how you should be. . . ." And even though this admonition can ring out any-where—that's probably why a truly bland, ugly landscape doesn't ex-ist as long as human beings haven't messed it up. I remember Suse once told me on the train to Lyon that nothing much was to be said for the area, that it was totally without charm. And I still remember that later on my walks, I found so much, much more than I had expected. I re-member a church on a hill, a low gray wall around a vineyard, a sunset between poplars. . . . But most particularly a gigantic, dark green, glittering grasshopper, which was like a finely turned bronze work of art. The gardeners and vintners would probably have had less enthu-siasm for the creature that was about the size of a dragonfly. I also know that I placed it in the palm of my hand where it remained totally still, and I showed it to my fellow students without eliciting much more than mild disgust. . . .

So, now I've arrived again on the subject of animals—my Hebrew teacher would say, "Of course!" I had given her during our second les-son a short speech on the topic of "Our Animals" to which she re-marked in the end that she didn't have the foggiest notion about such things. Since then her attitude toward me in this regard resembles that of Hugo Weinschenk toward the musically gifted Gerda Budden-brooks. He asks her at every encounter: "Well, how is the violin?" "Well, what are you going to tell me today? Something about animals again?"

Have I ever told you that I've been taking Hebrew conversation since the beginning of April? A suitable teacher lives just around the corner from us. She tells me that in twenty years of teaching, her stu-dents never advanced far enough to make conversation. And as a result, I "perpetrated" my first Hebrew poem yesterday, May 14, at the end of my fifth lesson. I'm going to recite it to her next time. It may still be full of mistakes, but I'm as proud as Sabine will be when she will have written her first correct word. Or maybe she did already? Our primer begins with "ei" "eis." . . .

It's a pity, more than a pity even, that I was not there to see her first steps in this new area. . . . She is probably much more adept than I

with the "i." By the way, I don't remember this ordeal at all; but Vati
can tell a story about it. . . .

Did I tell you about the cultural association evening, or better,
afternoon? "Jewish Word and Jewish Sound—Songs and Poems."
Mrs. Feld featured my work rather prominently. The recitation of two
of my poems was her best performance. And yet, it all did not touch
me that deeply; there is probably too much else going on in the mind
and heart. . . .

Speaking of "household": Look here, if Thea puts her room only
halfway in order so that it looks in our eyes like the Wild West, this is
probably by the standards of the country highly orderly and "true to
style"; but when not everything is in the right place in your electric
kitchen, it will appear sloppy and "contrary to style." Our new property in Finkenkrug never looked neglected; our old, landscaped garden sometimes did. Betty, about whom we speak a lot these days, once
said, for a similar reason, that her small, new apartment was not less
work for the maid than her house in the Westend. . . .

Thank you for the card of the seventh of the month. Yes, Thea's letter arrived. We passed along your various, small orders to Peter yesterday morning; he stopped by after a long time.—

What else? Nothing more—except best wishes from the heart for
both of you. Write again to your sister when you have a moment.

TRUDE

22

Berlin, July 14, 1940

Dear Hilde,

Your letter gave me great pleasure, especially the Rilke verses. I've
been rereading them since quite frequently. You did well to copy especially these verses for me. Of course, I know that the *Letters from Muzot* contain much else that is beautiful, compelling, and significant. A
woman I know, who owned them for years, would turn to various passages and recommend that I read them. I believe one shouldn't borrow
such a book like a novel, which one can read all the way through from

beginning to end, be done with, and give back. But this book, one should own so that one can sink into it periodically. So I thought I would ask for it for my birthday (since I always had a lack of birthday wishes anyway), but then I never did for various reasons; the main reason being that I counted on having to part with all my books sooner or later, and I didn't want to make new friends I would so soon lose again. When I was passing a window display, I saw a little Insel book, *The Song of the Fathers* by Edzard Schaper; the title appealed to me so much. Then I thought that the contents might be disappointing as I had found so often to be the case with beautifully titled works—but good, then I would conceive of a new contents with the same title. At one time, I had hoped from the words *Out of the Darkness* by Per Hallström something different than the Parisian bohème story I got to read. I simply "annexed" the beautiful title and created my own poem in *Welten*. Plagiarizers do it the other way around. They may dispossess the contents of somebody's work and only the title is their own. So I sacrificed the eighty pfennig and acquired the little book—and was rewarded in the most beautiful way. It is a narrative taken from the life of the Russian faith, the church, the monks; meanwhile, I passed it on to the woman mentioned; she was as surprised and enthusiastic as I was and her husband even more. All this written in the manner of sub specie aeternitas . . .

You can see from my letter that I'm by no means surprised that you should gradually be leaning toward "abstract" things (it may be that these are unjustly called so). Thinkers and poets (you see I count you among them too) have always, in times of great changes, held to the constant, timeless—the "don't-step-on-my-circles!" which Archimedes called out to the Roman soldiers. Speaking of "circles," we have here now a quite close circle that "rounds" itself every few weeks. Among them is the woman I mentioned above, then a painter and her husband, a philosopher, a well-known, eminent artist, and occasionally also his wife, who is a nice person but doesn't quite fit in with the rest of us, another woman who is an Egyptologist (she used to work in the field and was formerly a member of the Commission of the Berlin Egyptian Museum), also her sister, a graphic artist and teacher, and I. When we are together, the conversation rarely turns to current events but rather to topics of timeless interest. One afternoon I arrived late, and I found the men already engaged in a dispute over the question

"Christ or Buddha?" Although friendly, the fervor of the discussion might, in the opinion of many people, have been "worthy of a better cause." Sometimes we read to each other from our "collected" works. Although I'm always a bit skeptical of limp praise from friends, none of us suffers from vanity of the mind, and we speak openly if we dislike something and take the criticism and are thus guarded against what the late Marshal Lyautey called the French General Staff, "une société d'admiration mutuelle." It seems somewhat peculiar to me today, by the way, that I used this expression of "mutual admiration" already before the decisive events of the French campaign in a letter to a young South German poetess, since artists, when they are not plagued by mutual envy, succumb especially to the danger of mutual incense sprinkling. This young poetess—she is about fifteen years younger than I—wrote to me after a poetry reading that featured poems by both of us. She said she had my book but would like to get to know more of my poems and would I send her some to copy. This I did, and we have remained in contact ever since. But the whole affair makes me somewhat uneasy. She is, no doubt, very talented—in part, still promise, and in part, fulfillment already—her personality seems completely different from mine. Basically, this wouldn't bother me in and of itself. What goes against my grain is her insistence on addressing me as this great "animal wonder," this "respected model" and "master." First, I'm not a suitable object for something like this, and second, it doesn't go together with her otherwise refreshing, straightforward way of speaking without mincing words. Well, we are still in the beginning stages of our friendship—though I already received five letters from her—perhaps this newly planted tree will bear fruit someday. . . .

I continue to enjoy my language lessons, and recently I wrote another poem. This is the first with more than curiosity value and is not just like the "Snow and splendor and sunshine" of a famous poetess (do you know her?). It is called "Ha Zav," the toad. Of course, said my teacher, when I told her the title. Nevertheless, she declared one line to be stylistically quite innovative and worthy of a Bialik. She is a great admirer of Bialik, and this is her highest praise. My rhymes, however, were not quite on the level, and I'm putting forth great effort to improve them.—May I hear more about your own writings? Judging from the "Greek Travels," I don't believe that it is all as clumsy and worthless as you claim. However, you are probably right when you say that "it is probably impossible to create that which exists as long as one is so deeply involved, as long as one does not, and cannot, stand above it." The great writings about Napoleon were created only after St. Helena. From my own experience, I know that the subjects I choose for my poetry are more often drawn from the past, things that are distant rather than contemporary and near. I believe I've made in my letters the analogy with Impressionist paintings. To the close observer, they represent a chaotic mass of dots and only at a distance is the "real" picture revealed. And yet, do you really write exclusively about your "now" and not sometimes also about things that are already part of your "once," from which you have already gained a certain distance? By the way, I too have always found the night and morning hours to be the most productive—the evenings only when I didn't feel too exhausted. The same goes for winter afternoons, which is already evening anyway—I hardly ever created anything during daytime hours even if I had, as during summer vacations, plenty of time. Of course, I was unable to accomplish anything at all with the typewriter on my knees. I know that for some famous writers, paper, pencil, pen, and the like, in short the tools of the trade, play an important role; for me, they are secondary, and I have used them only when the actual act of creation was already behind me. The typewriter especially . . . It comes only at the very end for the final, clean copy. This is why it is harder for me to make big changes in a typewritten text than it is for others. To sit down and type my work from my head directly into the machine would be, I believe, impossible for me. Until now I was not even able to write a letter that way—if it is to be worth something, I always have to reach for the pen. This is the first one I did differently for reasons of saving space, and I don't know how successful it is. But, of course, this is not meant as a value judgment that applies to others. I almost believe that you write better with the machine than with the pen. . . .

Enough now of this long epistle; I still have another letter to write.

To
Sabine Wenzel

My dear Monster!

For you, I shall widen the lines a little. You may not be able to read whole words yet, but maybe at least individual letters. I thank you for the tree picture; it was really beautiful. I won't write a poem about it but a very long story. Right now I don't have much time to do that, so it will be quite a while before it'll be ready. I already know the beginning of the story: The trees are on an island in the middle of the ocean near Africa, an island without people, only plants and animals. I recently wrote a story forty pages long. Actually, I wanted to send it to your Mutti. Flora was in this story. Do you remember Flora? Helene, who says hello, went to Finkenkrug the other day to see Wally in the little house. She also visited Mrs. Zerbe, to whom we gave Flora and Jacki; both are still alive! Jacki still runs around with the chickens the way he used to do. Flora, unfortunately, had an injured foot from stepping on some broken glass. Opa also says hello. He won't sign here since he already sent a special letter to both of you in the middle of the week.

Now stay well and be good, and if you are naughty sometimes—a child has to be naughty, right, so that Mutti isn't bored with the constantly good behavior—so if you are naughty sometimes, don't do it for too long. And continue your beautiful drawing—when I was a child, I couldn't draw at all. I remember we schoolchildren had a big drawing pad each, and we were supposed to draw an Easter egg with charcoal; just couldn't do it. I tried several times, and the art teacher, as you can imagine, was very dissatisfied with me. I tried several times again, even when I was grown-up, to draw something also with ink or paint, but I never succeeded. Until one day, it occurred to me to cut silhouettes of small figures, animals, landscapes, from black paper: that I could do. So I'm not totally unskilled in those arts. . . .

Now this is enough. With much love, as much as always,

AUNT TRUDE

Attached is the requested dedication! I still remember that it was about "Die Fremde," but I don't remember the exact words of the dedication. If you care for the "Urtext," then you have to send it to me for copying. But I presume it doesn't make that much difference to you exactly how it is worded. The date too I can't remember. That's why it is missing.

P.S. Peter wrote again and sent pictures. He is well.

23

August 11, 1940

Dear Hilde,

How I would have liked to have "spread" myself out a little had it not been for a long letter I just wrote to that young poetess I wrote to you about and were it not for the fact that this letter must be posted. This exchange of letters has improved since she no longer makes any of her little literary inquiries, which I didn't like answering at all. This "master/disciple relationship," even if unspoken, is not for me. Lately we have been writing about animals. . . . This morning I visited Lindenheims in their new apartment; it is much better there for them. From Peter, we receive frequent and good news. He hopes that in a better moment, he will receive a longer letter from you sometime.

TRUDE

Greetings for Pipkin.

24

August 12, 1940

Dear Hilde,

Against all expectations this letter is still here after all, and so I can "spread" myself out a little more as I had intended. Of course, writing becomes easier if one has a letter from the other person before one's physical or mental eye—like a ball of yarn from which one pulls the thread to start knitting along. Such a ball of yarn I don't have from you today, but I'll make do without. I'll have to spin my yarn by myself then. Shall we start with the reading material? What have I read last? For quite some time, only the extensive Lavater book by Mary Lavater-Sloman, almost every night in bed one or two chapters—this is against my usual habits; but I never got around to it during the day. This very stimulating work is filled with so much labor, it deserves to be studied more leisurely and with a clearer, rested head than I have been able to bring to it. But I always like to return borrowed books as soon as possible even if, as in this case, I received specific permission for a long-term loan. That's why I didn't want to put off reading it to a more convenient time. Such a time will come who knows when.

As for the trees, Püppi's painted trees meanwhile have begun to bloom in my imagination—and as soon as I'm "self-sufficient" with regard to writing poetry, I must, how cheap, deprive myself of the poetic productions of other producers. I believe I wrote that I have transplanted these trees to an island of my creation, the Isle of Arlat in the Indian Ocean (discovered in the year 1743 by the also self-created French seafarer Arlat du Moutier). However, after I animated it with all kinds of plants and animals, the island has meanwhile sunk back into the sea. All I saved were the trees, and I'm just now in search of a new place in which to plant. At the moment, I'm traveling back and forth between the region around Ebermergen (Nördlingen, Donauwörth) and the area around Bad Pyrmont (Höxter, Hameln). Maybe I'll mix the two regions in a future story. We'll see. I'm curious how it will all turn out, almost as if I had no part in this new creation myself. After all, it is something that "comes over" a person. . . . As I wrote in my last letter, I'd like to know more about your writing, of which you only give a hint now and then.

Speaking of writing and poetry, would you do me a favor? Really only a small one, if the volume of *Welten* is not too far out of reach. In rereading this collection recently, I discovered a dumb typo in the poem "Borzoi." It does not immediately appear as such, but I'd like you to correct it anyway. At the bottom of line 22, it says, "und hebst mir dein Frauenantlitz mit jener Milde der Hündin, des Einhorns entgegen" [and you lift your female countenance with that certain languish of the female hound, the unicorn toward me]; this should read "Hindin" [hind], not "Hündin" [female dog]. Would you, if, as I said, *Welten* is not too far stashed away, insert an "i" for the "ü"? Otherwise, there will be for a hundred years to come a dispute among scholars whether the place cited commands the authority of the "Swiss manuscript" or of the existing fragments of the "Berlin transcription." There is a poem by Fontane about which something like this is going on today. . . . I believe that the whole back and forth was caused by a mere mistake on the part of the poet in the course of writing it down. This happens also among poets and is by no means a rare occurrence.

Excuse the exclusive "shop talk" of this letter. Some other time about other things. Our outward life follows the usual course. Helene says hello and hopes to write again soon. And as I said, if you should have a good hour, then send a few typewritten pages to

TRUDE

August 13, 1940

My dear Meisterchen,

I would, of course, be happy to hear what Mrs. Lavater has to say about Trudchen's poems.

VATI

And, in case Mrs. L. would like to see the little volume of poems, or if you think it's appropriate, then feel free to show her any printed or manuscript material you have.

TRUDE

25

August 20, 1940

My dear Meisterchen!

[. . .] We just received a long letter from Thea. She writes, incomprehensibly to me and doubtful, that you are playing with the idea of sending our dear, one and only Bienelein alone away to Fritz. I'm unable to grasp your reasons from here, and it is difficult for me to give you advice, but I must say that you should be very careful when it comes to Fritz since he is very self-centered and unscrupulous. [. . .]

Dear Hilde,

Just a few words to let you know that I share Vati's reservations completely; indeed, I have even greater reservations toward Fritz than he has. You may say that we should go packing with our negative advice, if we don't have anything positive to give; but . . . the matter is too important to keep what we know from you. Maybe you don't have a choice. . . .

Best regards from the heart!

TRUDE

26

Berlin W., September 11, 1940

Dear Hilde,

I won't respond in detail to your last letter concerning Sabine's "great journey" since Vati answered that already. I'm sorry if we caused you such consternation; but Thea's letter caused us much consternation as well—and as you saw from my letter, I guessed that you had to act the way you did. I'd rather speak of something more pleasant today: of your wonderful, long letter to me. You know, before it arrived, I had taken your previous long letter [without date and beginning with a citation from Rilke—from a Muzot letter] from my desk to read it again. Letters like that cannot be read only once. . . .

How shall I begin? I just see on page two the name Julian Green. Since Dora Benjamin gave me *Adrienne Mesurat* as a present (Walter had great admiration for J. G.), I have read almost everything by him; most I own. Of his five novels, the last two, *Minuit* and *Epaves,* are of lesser quality. The middle work, *Leviathan,* perhaps the most stimulating and suspenseful, tends a bit toward genre. The first two works, *Mont-Cinère* and *Adrienne Mesurat,* by contrast, cannot be praised enough. I know them by heart and am unable to decide which one deserves the prize (maybe the second after all). Such density, such cohesion of the whole that is nowhere interrupted, such absence of anything extraneous, anything haphazard, such sparsity of surface action and concentration of internal events, and, in *Adrienne Mesurat,* a maximum of the erotic with a minimum of the sexual. At this moment, I can name few novelists who are his equal. However, I noticed that J. G. is apparently very difficult to translate; the language, as well as the entire work, does not make the same original, wonderful impression in German. . . . What have you read meanwhile?

Niels Lyhne—I picked it up a while ago. Strange, this book, which you love so much, used to be so remote from me, and even today, it has not become any closer. I cannot say why this is so. Maybe because I sense a persuasive fin-de-siècle mood about it. I'm always reminded of fallen, wilting leaves in the autumn. . . . maybe the work foreshadows the early death of the writer. . . . But actually, a breath of melancholy is not something that leaves me untouched elsewhere—I cannot explain why *Niels Lyhne* doesn't touch me more deeply. Maybe because I cannot find anything of myself in any of the characters. Rilke, by contrast, is very close to me. Critics have claimed to detect his influence in my poetry. They are mistaken. I became acquainted with Rilke (with the exception of the "Cornet") so late that he was no longer able to influence my development. Here Lessing's saying in *Laocoön* becomes applicable—one artist seems to be imitating another because they share the same models. And I did have the same models: the great French lyrical works; also the influence of Slavic writers is present.

Since you're living in this landscape . . . I don't think you will ever lose it if you once truly possessed it. That which sinks from us, vanishes, are things we have only seen with a superficial glance; before the inner eye, nothing dissolves so easily. It seems to me too that the beauty of a piece of earth is something very personal, something as personal as the beauty of a woman who leaves one man untouched and arouses another. . . . Do you remember by any chance the passage in Geijerstam's *Thora* where the husband shows his young wife the beauty of his homeland, which makes no impression on Thora because she doesn't love him? Sometimes a miserable farm can be the most beautiful spot in the world. . . . But Wöllishofen is no run-down farm (very important to state that, isn't it?); after all, I hold the heretical view that you have to bring something to all the wonders before your eyes, and for that reason, they are yours alone, even if they will eventually lose something of their full color and strength and become somewhat faded. . . . "In later summer, everything is a gift," you write. Yes, late, that is also true for the late summer of life. Mine was as rich as my spring once was and gave me more happiness. . . .

I just saw two bees crawling over the pink florets of the stonecrop in the flower box on the balcony. It sounds ridiculous, but I'm so deeply touched by their sight—it seems to me that I haven't seen a bee for an unthinkably long time. Their buzzing spoke to me somehow of all that is green, flowering, growing, fruit bearing, all things that I miss here.

When I think of bees [*Bienen*], I think, of course, of Bienelein [Sabine]—her wish to become a great dancer has Aunt Trude's full approval. You know how much I love the art of dance—in this connection, I dug out my old collection of program notes and remembered. . . . And I see one bill already before me: "Only performance of the most famous ballerina . . . (of which country?) . . . Sabine Wenzel . . ." And the order of presentation? As "Dying Swan" (Anna Pavlova) or "Antique Epitaph" (Charlotte Bara), I cannot yet picture Püppi. But how about "Dance of the Little Goats" or a "Spring" or a "Butterfly" with music by Grieg of the same name? I know another dance accompanied by tambourine, rattle, recorder, in short a so-called children's orchestra—"The Little Monster" and another "Of the Sleeping Apple." I imagine (and may be wrong, of course) that Bienelein will be a dancer like Grete Wiesenthal, whom I only know from pictures and descriptions. It seems to me, there is something refreshing, gay, unburdened, something summery, reminiscent of summer vacations that lives in her dance. . . . I just remember. There is something similar in the dancing of Lucy Dieselhausen—and I have seen her more than once. In her enchanting, grotesque dance "Dimmy-Dommy" (I still have the tune in my ear), I can well imagine a somewhat more grown Sabine.

So now I have spoken for a while only of "frivolous things" like dances and dancers; but are these really frivolities? Hardly. The beauty of dance is an art form and as such it is great and eternal. But, another question. Are you in a mood to read about words like "dimmy-dommy" (I just tried out the dancing steps in my room as much as I can remember) and "Dying Swan"? Maybe three days ago, yes, and in the last two days, no . . . Separated as we are, the correspondent easily runs the risk of catching the addressee in an inconvenient moment, be it that the latter already has another visitor or that he is disturbed at a moment of great "inner house cleaning." But I don't want to wreck my brain with searching for a different writing topic because of such considerations, and another one may not be the right one either, nor do I want to put down my pen prematurely.

By the way, I'm at the moment like someone whose appetite is whetted by reading about oysters and champagne and caviar; I have written myself actually into a hunger for dance, and I yearn to be able to see once again a great ballerina. My last one was Mary Wigman. Shall I wait for Sabine? . . .

It's getting dark. . . . be well. Again thanks for the beautiful letter; let another one follow soon. And best regards to you and the great ballerina

From

(AUNT) TRUDE

P.S. Vati wants you to know he received a letter from Mrs. Lavater. She would be glad if you would give her a call in Winterthur.

27

October 7, 1940

Dear Hilde,

Thank you very much for the postcards of September 17 and 26. Concerning the letter you promised, I can only say "the sooner the better." But at any rate, I will be able to look forward to it and be patient. The Moles received a letter from Thea. Since the first of September, she is giving religious instruction to a class of thirteen children (ten of the children are from long-established families). She began with the creation of the world since these children never had any religious training, and in Spanish. Most fluent in this language is the big son; nobody notices that this is not his native tongue when he speaks. Otherwise, he has grown sixteen centimeters, and his leg continues to improve. The Junge apparently didn't go to see his friend Helmut but went to join Margot. Thea knew no details about it since he was still en route.

I'd like to hear more about Püppi's visit to the museum. Be well, both of you!

TRUDE

28

Berlin, October 27, 1940

My dear Monster, Bienelein, and Püppi!

I wish you a very happy birthday. Do you remember how you all used to sing at Aunt Ilse's: "I'm happy that I was born and have a birthday today . . ."? Now, I want to continue on the typewriter; otherwise, it takes too long. I won't be able to fit everything I have to tell you on the paper. There is much I have to tell you. All right, what do I wish you? Well, I want to wish you something that gives me something also. I wish that you will become a great ballerina. I have not seen a great ballerina in a long time, and so I will be able to see one again in that case. I'm looking forward to it already.

One day all advertisement pillars will be covered with green or yellow or blue posters: "Only performance by the famous ballerina Sabine Wenzel—Old and New Dances." The tickets are very expensive; but when a famous dancer like Sabine Wenzel gives her only dance performance, she can command money for it. . . . And Aunt Trude will get a free ticket, won't she? So, I'm sitting in my seat; it's a very good one, first tier, third row in the middle—the hall is already quite full, but more and more people are entering. They are all in formal festive dress in honor of Sabine Wenzel. People are talking—a great jumble of voices—suddenly the bell, all fall silent and take a quick glance at the program bill. There it lists the first item: "Dance of the Snowflake."

The second bell, the hall darkens, the curtain rises, the stage is in plain view, brightly lit. The stage is not very big, the decor is simple, the floor is covered with a gray blue cloth, and all around, enclosing the stage, are gray blue curtains. But it is still empty. Another moment . . . then the music begins to play softly, a violin, a flute. And almost simultaneously, the ballerina steps out from behind the curtains. Sabine Wenzel. She wears a light, soft, loose dress of white silk and white tulle with swan down trimming and white stockings and white silk slippers. And she begins to dance. . . . She dances the snowflake, which filters down from the sky, carried and whirled about by the wind until it finally falls to the ground. Now it lies there, collapsed. . . . the last note of the music fades. . . . the audience waits another minute, not knowing if the dance is really over, and then they begin to clap. . . . And Sabine Wenzel, the snowflake, revives, gets up quickly, takes a bow, and with soft steps, she disappears between the curtains, without a sound, as she had entered. For a few minutes, the stage remains empty—Sabine Wenzel to make a costume change for the second dance—meanwhile, the music continues to play so that the audience will not get bored. Then follows the second dance: "Reseda." Sabine Wenzel appears in a Biedermeier dress with a mighty fluffed up, very wide shirt of reseda green, faded green of stiff silk with little gold ornaments. In her hand is a large fan of peacock feathers. This time she moves in high-heel rose beetle shoes. She moves very slowly, festively, in a very old-fashioned, awkward dance with many bows and curtsies. Her hair too is made up in Biedermeier style, parted in the middle and long corkscrew curls on both sides of the ears. The audience likes this dance too, and when it ends with a low bow from the ballerina, there is applause all around. I can hardly recount all the dance pieces that are still to come, and there are many. . . .

In one dance, which arouses particular enthusiasm among the audience, Sabine Wenzel is dressed as a Dutch girl, with a little white cap and a red pleated skirt, and she taps around in wooden shoes. The music accompanies her with the song: "Dance, Püppi, dance, I'll give you a hen. . . ." Following this dance, after Sabine Wenzel has again disappeared between the curtains in the back of the stage, the front curtain falls suddenly at the same time as the stage darkens, and the next moment, the lights go on in the hall—it is brilliantly illuminated.

Intermission.

People in the audience leave their seats (so does Aunt Trude). They stream through the open doors of the hall into the corridors where they walk about to stretch their legs after sitting so long and to cool off from the heat inside the hall. They eat bonbons and chocolate; some even brought butter sandwiches, and while they are eating, they talk about the great dancer who was once again, in every dance, "fabulous" "wonderful" "fantastic." Aunt Trude hears some of what they are saying and tries to remember so she can tell her niece Sabine about it after the performance. (Mutti is not of the party since she already knows all the dances from another performance in another town.)

The bell rings, and all the people hurry back to their seats. They are hardly seated when the bell rings again, the hall darkens, and the stage brightens again. The violins begin to play; again, Sabine Wenzel appears. And in the second part, she dances her most famous creation, the dance that had made her famous all over the world and aroused the enthusiasm of audiences in every town and country. It is called "The Little Monster." For this dance she had designed herself a very strange costume of thin, soft fabric, fitting skintight and covering her entire body to the neck and also the arms and legs; it is gray brown, gray green, with scarlet red polka dots. Is it a toad skin or a lizard dress? A tightly fitting cap of the same color is pulled over her hair and ears, and now she begins to dance—not at all like a human being, no, like a strange creature, well just like a little "monster," sometimes cheerful, sometimes sad—one must have seen it; it is indescribable. And suddenly applause bursts forth; the audience claps as in a frenzy; they climb on their seats and wave their handkerchiefs and call out "bravo" like crazy. And Sabine Wenzel stands there in her monster costume and takes a bow again and again, both arms filled with flower bouquets which had been presented to her by enthusiastic gentlemen: Japanese gold stripe lilies, pin carnations, yellow and red roses. . . . Now she wants to leave; the performance is over, and she is tired from all that dancing. But the audience creates a gigantic ruckus and refuses to leave despite a warning from the ushers—it is useless, Sabine Wenzel must dance "The Little Monster" one more time. . . . Then everything is finally really over. The audience leaves; people get their coats and hats; the stage darkens; so does the hall after the ushers have cleaned up a little. Sabine Wenzel, in her dressing room, puts on her street clothes, wraps herself in her evening coat, descends into the street where her limousine is waiting and drives home with all her flower bouquets. At home, Mutti is waiting up for her at this late hour. Mutti and all the friends, who hear about it later, are happy about her success, most of all, however,

YOUR AUNT TRUDE

Is this a fairy tale or a true story?—

Opa received Mutti's letter of the twenty-third with all enclosures. He was very happy about it and sent off the card to Mrs. Pakscher.

29

November 19, 1940

Dear Hilde,

Thank you very much for your beautiful, long letter, which I plan to answer soon in greater detail. I always carry it with me when I go shopping; when I have to wait in line somewhere, I pull it out and read it for the umpteenth time. I'm pleased that Sabine enjoyed my letter. I enjoyed it myself, imagining the dance evening so vividly. I'm sure that came through in the narration. Judging from the picture, Sabine has really been shooting up. Not at all the roly-poly anymore she used to be . . . To her and you greetings from Trude

30

Berlin, November 24, 1940

Dear Hilde,

I started writing Friday morning to thank you for the letter. I started out by telling you that I had picked up once again my Tauchnitz volume of the Conrad stories [*Youth, Heart of Darkness, The End of the Rope*— the latter a story of a sea captain who is losing his eyesight, it may not have been translated], but after a short attempt of reading these stories, I put them away again. Stimulated by your letter, I tried it again, with the same lack of success. I don't really know why when I first read these stories years ago, they left a deep impression on me. Now I picked up the great Lawrence novel *The Plumed Serpent* (it is probably still awaiting translation). The setting is among the Indians and half-Indians of Mexico, and the heroine is a white woman who "rode away." And what do you know, with Conrad I failed, and with Lawrence I had a good journey. I do have some explanations for this difference, answers to the why of the whole thing—in short, this might have offered an opportunity for a quite animated literary discussion. But I left off writing the letter after I had started it. Now, I'm not really in the mood for literary discussions. The mood I'm in . . . if it were a physical matter, I would describe this condition as pregnancy. And that's probably what it is in a spiritual sense. I'm carrying right now an elephant child; as far as I know, the female elephant carries its young about two years. Who knows I may carry it even longer in the end. . . .

The story behind this "it" is the following: Did I tell you that the teacher with whom I had studied Hebrew conversation for four months went away? I've been searching for a replacement and accompanied one of our housemates to an advanced course offered by the community at the Lehmann School (Joachimsthalerstrasse). I scrounged around there; that is, I attended a lesson as a "silent participant," but it was still too rudimentary for me. At the end of the lesson, the teacher exchanged a few words with me and then mentioned to my housemate that I was probably best suited for a course for teachers. This consists only of conversation among teachers so that their knowledge doesn't get rusty. The man's assessment of my Hebrew was probably too high, and I would hardly be able to follow such a conversation. But I want to try it at any rate after the beginning of the New Year. And now, the teacher's suggestion has put big ideas into my head. . . .

I probably mentioned already that I've written a few poems in Hebrew, which my teacher, after countless corrections, declared ready for print. Be that as it may, I know only too well that these poems, even if not literally, are still in the strictest sense transcriptions from German and that a real Hebrew poem should look and sound very different. Fortunately, it is not the case that a poet can and must speak only in his mother tongue, else I would have no hope of ever writing poetry in the language of our fathers. Absolutely not; poets of foreign origin have often enriched the art of their new homeland with sounds and colors which "natives" would never have found. (Conrad was, as you know, a Polish aristocrat by birth.) As far as Hebrew is concerned, there is the added feature that nowhere in Europe was it, until recently, anybody's first language, at most the second . . . in areas where Yiddish was the first . . . But it is a difference whether somebody speaks flawless German, French, English and adds a certain charm through a slight tinge, a pinch of the exotic, or whether the expression is awkward and completely un-German, un-French, or un-English. And my Ivrit still belongs to the latter variety. Of course, I have cause for feeling reassured. Tchernikovsky's poems in my little book sound almost as if they had all been translated from the German, and a few of Bialik's minor poems are of Russian origin.—And the elephant child? Well, the elephant child is this: I know now how a Hebrew poem should not be, how I must not write, and I feel now that I will soon know how I must write it, and this poem, which does not yet exist (the unborn), is taking form within me. It may take months or years, and I hope it won't be a miscarriage despite all its likely defects. . . . that's why I have not done anything in German lately.

I'm just thinking of Bosy. It's strange; since you no longer have the store, he has become more distant for me, I can hardly imagine that he could move away any farther. He had been so closely identified with the store that it seems for me that only now did the store—at long last—die. . . . the store is no more. I don't know if I'm making myself understood, what I mean. . . .

Lindenheims were visiting yesterday afternoon to say good-bye. If all goes well, they will leave on Wednesday and travel via Aachen, Paris, Irún, San Sebastián to Lisbon; from there they will set sail on December 3. I feel about them the way I have lately been feeling about all people who are saying good-bye. There's already a distance between us, but I don't feel that they are the ones emigrating; it is I who is departing and they who are staying behind. . . .

Uncle Alex was astounded and almost indignant, and Aunt Lindenheim was outright insulted when I made the admittedly heretical remark that my longing was not directed toward Montevideo, not at all toward America. . . . Lawrence said in *The Plumed Serpent:* "And sometimes she asked herself whether America was the great continent of death, the great no to the European and Asiatic and African yes. Was it really the great melting pot in which people from the creative continents would be melted down, not into a new creation but into the uniformity of death? Was it the great continent of ruin and all its inhabitants the executors of mystical destruction? Did it pluck, pluck so long on man's created soul until the growing seed had been plucked out and left him as a mechanical creature with automatic reaction? . . . the continent that destroys what other continents had created. The continent whose spatial mind only struggles to gouge the eyes from God's countenance. Was that America?"

Maybe Lawrence is wrong, and this is not what America is. Perhaps . . . But even if my rational mind doesn't agree with him simply and without reservation, my feeling says he is right. And almost all I have heard and read of late about America (the exceptions confirm the rule) seems to say he is right. By no means to America, if possible. My face is turned toward the East, toward the southeast. . . .

Tolstoy's word is golden: but around the gold still smolder the cinders. Cinders I call this, so that those who expect the artist, the worker of the mind, to starve in an unheated garret can and will misuse it. For otherwise, he would live the life of a parasite which, as Tolstoy says, serves only false art, only false science. One must guard him from that. . . .

Be well for now. Vati sends his love to both of you; Helene too says hello to both "ladies," and last from the heart

TRUDE

31

December 5, 1940

Dear Hilde!

Meanwhile you must have received my long letter of the twenty-fourth—I wrote myself completely out, and right now the reservoir is empty. I'm sure Mrs. Lavater's Russian is probably better than mine. I read *War and Peace* in translation more than twenty years ago. But I do own Tolstoy's *Folk Tales* and "Hadji Murat" in the original language. (It just occurred to me that I should read this one again sometime. . . .) I already suspected that Mrs. L. was from Hamburg since the shipping family Sloman, to which she surely belongs, is well known there. That you're ready to break your sworn promise not to write any more letters on my behalf is very pleasing to

YOUR TRUDE

Regards to Püppi.

32

Berlin, December 15, 1940

Dear Hilde,

My heartfelt thanks for the letter and the picture—even though the monster really looks monstrous with the twisted face! That's probably due to the sun. We think that she generally has a tendency to make faces, to squint, which is probably due to the weakness of her eyes. (I had a tendency to squint with my nearsighted right eye when I was a child.) Couldn't you get her to wear her glasses regularly, especially since, as you wrote, the doctor recommends it? You could tell her that Aunt Trude had to do that for a year or two when she was young and that it was very good for her. (I was then at an age, the teenage years, when it was much more uncomfortable for a girl to be forced to walk around as a spectacle snake, than it would be for a child; but then I placed so little stock in my "beauty." . . .) You could also tell her, or maybe you shouldn't, that she writes almost as well as her Mutti. The pleasures which you wish me, such pleasures, those that correspond to my nature, do occur from time to time, and if not very often, then more often than at one time, more frequently than when I was in my twenties. It is not that I have learned to be more modest and that I'm bending over to glean that which I once would have carelessly trammeled. That too is possible in human nature; but resignation has never been my virtue nor my weakness. Neither did I belong to those who gather many small joys from which to build a great joy, like a bouquet of flowers. For me, there had to appear the great, the one joy, the absolute happiness, a sun from which lesser joys radiate. This sun may be covered with clouds right now, veiled in fog, hidden in night; and yet, I know that it is irremovably there, a fixed star rather than a moving planet. I also know, however, that many people are like the horseman in the fairy tale of the "Three Feathers." Since his horse says every time "Don't pick the feather off the ground," he leaves the first and second feather he comes across untouched. When he comes to the third, he dismounts and picks it up despite the horse's warning. So he becomes king; but had he not taken the third feather, he would have found a fourth one on top of the mountain and would have become emperor. Few people wait for the fourth feather; most don't make it to the third but must gather immediately the first or second they come across since they are afraid that they will have to travel for a long time without discovering another. And that is really the way it is. One cannot, with certainty, hold out the hope to somebody who left the first untouched so the second may be found, let alone more.

What do I wish you? Maybe your time of horseback riding and feather searching is already over; in the end, the best that I wish you, can wish you, is again your own business. A business, that is, a task, a living space, a force field in the literal sense of the word. That would be a feather too, one of the last on the way to the top. . . .

My birthday, as you guessed, was very quiet: no relatives came, and my acquaintances knew nothing of the day. Thea and Peter wrote (nothing worth reporting though). Only one present I asked from Vati and did receive it, the *Letters from Muzot.* I'm reading them in the evenings; they are a true treasure. If one wanted to nitpick, find something to criticize, one could say something against the "sprinklings" of French (métier, *désastre,* etc.); I must admit they bother me a little bit. I concur with Emperor Augustus, who spoke excellent Greek but prohibited himself and others, exactly for that reason, to decorate Latin speech with sprinkles of Greek. Another objection would be perhaps that the letters are too "beautiful," too "precious" that they are not really letters but works of art. (Question: can and should letters be works of art?) But Rilke was an artist with every pulse beat, not only when he happened to be writing poetry, not only in those short hours of being in a state of levitation—as are the rest of us. I read last night—and I was happy to learn that he had a greyhound in his coat of arms. I was reminded of my Flora and thought that she would have inspired him; as in the case of "The Panther" and "The Swan," a poem might have sprouted in him: "The Greyhound" . . .

And "coats of arms are extraordinarily expressive to me, one could draw much from them and tell the truth much better than has been attempted. . . ." (no. 26). In another letter is a playful reference to "little monsters" (does he too mean children?). May your and your little monster's days be as good as possible and greetings from the heart to both of you

From

TRUDE

33

December 23, 1940

Dear Hilde,

Here is a little story—also for Püppi—which I meant to tell you for some time, but I had so much else to write about. . . . A remembrance by the poet Bialik about his early school days. The teacher showed the little boy a card with the Hebrew letter "Aleph." "Do you see here the wooden yoke with two buckets?" "Yes, I see."—"Well, that is called 'Aleph.' Repeat: what is the name of this symbol?" "Marrusya," answered the child. As it happened, just at the moment when he recognizes the wooden yoke and the buckets, he also sees the Polish water carrier Marrusya, who handles such an instrument, and the teacher was helpless to persuade the child to connect the word "Aleph," which has no meaning for the pupil, with this symbol. Every time he is asked what this symbol is called, he answers: "Marrusya." Nevertheless, Bialik went on to become a great poet. . . . And Sabine, of whom I thought vividly when I read this recollection, even learned to read meanwhile. And even I can write the letter "i," which was not expected on the basis of my beginnings in school.

For the New Year, everything good and wonderful for both of you!

TRUDE

Helene sends best regards.

34

January 21, 1941

Dear Hilde,

Last night we took out the family pictures (which will go to you someday); Mrs. Horwitz, who is a visual artist and has an eye for such things, declared the other day that I was the spitting image of great-grandfather Schoenfliess; he didn't have a single feature or expression that I don't have, so she claims. I took out the pictures yesterday, and Peter agreed that it was true. Until now, nobody had ever noticed it, I myself least of all. In terms of character, I'm certainly very unlike my forebear; only my talent for languages, according to Mutti's testimony, I inherited from him. And it may be that the resemblance became more pronounced only with my advancing years. More, some other time.

Best regards to you and Püppi

TRUDE

35

January 27, 1941

Dear Hilde,

Meanwhile you should have received our various pieces of correspondence, also enclosed my two copies of poems. (It's a short cycle of four religious poems; three of them I sent to you previously; the fourth will follow sometime.) Today we received a letter from Thea, which made us very happy—she is as competent as ever. Teaches math and German. She received a letter from the Junge; he's well and the food is good. "Margot very much counts on all of us getting together there," she writes. Yesterday morning I visited, as a favor, Suse's Aunt Hedwig from Dessau, who lives here in a private home. She remembers you and Mutti visiting her shortly after the outbreak of the war in 1914; you were visiting at the same time as her mother, Aunt Sophie.
    Say hello to the little monster for me.

And greetings to you too, of course, and just as much from the heart

TRUDE

36

Berlin, March 9, 1941

Dear Hilde,

Peter shared with us your letter of late February—you can imagine that what you write about money matters was not very edifying for us to hear despite your good spirits. I don't want to comment too much on it; you are familiar with my opinion on this from past events: and that is, if one cannot help—and in this case not even give advice—it is useless to sound off with consolation speeches, be they adorned with the words of the poets or with biblical citations. . . . Of course, now and then, I depart from my principle, especially if a mere word, an encouraging word, can be of help. But, unfortunately, even my most beautiful sermon won't generate a single Swiss centime for you. I'm often reminded of a story in Buber's *Tales of the Hasidim.* A pious man tells his students that much evil also contains some good. Whereupon a student asks what good could be in denying God. The pious man answers: "If a poor man should ever come to you in his need, you shouldn't point to God; you shouldn't send him away with words of consolation from Scriptures; no, you may think: there is no God and nobody but I myself can help him." Of course, where physical want is accompanied by suffering of the soul, a good word is never out of place next to a good deed. . . .

I think it very unjust on the part of Papa to find fault with his daughter's spelling. Anybody can write "Spiele" [games] but "Sbile," only the little monster! That's something different for a change! And if you consider that she will spend seventy, perhaps eighty or ninety years, writing the word "Brief" [letter] with an "e," why then shouldn't she draw the word during one brief year of her life without an "e"? The main thing is for the child to maintain the pleasure she gets from writing and reading and to be encouraged in it. Homework should be supervised and corrected, yes. But when the child takes up a pencil for the fun of it, one should not carp about it; otherwise, fun turns into drudgery, and that would be a pity. . . . I remember an incident in a nursery school where I worked in 1914–15. I had given the children gray clay, and they were busy kneading away. Each child modeled something, without much instruction, whatever came to mind at the moment. Only one boy, who had come to us recently from the Pestalozzi-Fröbel House, sat helpless in front of his lump of clay. In answer to my question, he explained that he wasn't used to doing anything without a model. At the Pestalozzi-Fröbel House, they always had some object to copy. I placed a water pitcher in front of him, and he imitated the form—the whole afternoon—he worked very cleanly and orderly and with great effort, by "the sweat of his brow," I almost said. The other children played and enjoyed the game while they were at it. This boy worked and gained satisfaction from his work only after he finished everything. Behind the creations, in part unrecognizable, of the others was creative energy. This impeccably formed pitcher, however, was the work of a little copyist. . . . The boy had lost at his school the ability to draw without a model—hence my somewhat heretical view about nursery schools in general.

That you shouldn't remember Robertson hardly has anything to do with a poor memory; he was a coworker of the Junge and appeared in our life only after you had left for Switzerland, and you probably heard as little about him before as we did. We received several pieces of mail lately: (1) a card from Uncle Max; (2) a card from Lindenheims; (3) a letter from Thea. She writes that she and Wolfgang as well as the Junge and Margot are all doing well, and she thanks you for your December letter. Ls had a bad voyage (middle deck) but arrived well. Uncle Max and Aunt Grete moved to Montevideo, so Rudolf and Poldi are now alone on the farm. (I wonder how this will work out in the long run and whether one can count on a long run at all. . . .)

Write again a long letter when you have a chance. Not that I put much stock in whose "turn" it is, but your letters, aside from giving me great enjoyment, are the warp into which I can fling the shuttle with my yarn. Best greetings for both of you

TRUDE

Enclosed is the fourth and last poem of the "Zyklus" [cycle]! Helene sends regards. She just baked a little cake for Bienelein—too bad that one cannot tele-eat as with television and telephoning.

37

Berlin, May 18, 1941

Dear Hilde,

Thank you for your card of the eighth of this month—I surmised already that your long silence had something to do with the "side effects" of your move. By the way, we too have a move behind us, one under the motto: "Moving in your own home!" Since the beginning of

May, we have rented out the two rooms in the rear (one of them was mine), all furnished. And still, we had to move around several pieces of furniture, take some out, put in others, and change things generally. We had to empty the closets of our belongings and store them elsewhere. This required in part some thinking since we do not suffer from an excess of space in this apartment.

Just on the day you wrote, our tenants moved in: a retired district court judge from Glogau with his seventy-nine-year-old mother and her caretaker. As far as one can judge the situation within such a short time, we seem to have made a good choice. He's a cultured, refined, touchingly unprepossessing, yet quite unsophisticated, impractical man.

The caretaker is a pleasant, friendly person, and our common use of the kitchen takes place without a glitch—this, even though she uses right now all my cooking and eating utensils since her own have to be taken down from the attic first. But—the but lies temporarily in the fact that the mother, the widow of a high-ranking public health official [*Geheimer Medizinalrat* or *Sanitätsrat*] has not yet joined them. The old lady fell two days before they moved in as she was getting up in the morning and broke her arm. She was taken to a hospital, and there she fell out of bed a second time, this time unfortunately on her head. She's on the way to recovery and will probably be released into home care and will be brought here. But all these last few days, the son and the caretaker have been running back and forth between the apartment and the hospital; often they spent the night there, and their restlessness and excitement touched us, of course, as well, especially since it came from people we liked. With the hopefully continuing improvement of the old lady, it will, I think, get quieter around here. . . .

By the way, the judge was born in Briesen which makes him a landsman of Uncle Alex; he's also familiar with the hotel. The caretaker is from Thorn, and one of her teachers in school was a Miss Lau. I don't know if you remember; the Laus, three sisters and a brother, lived in a little house diagonally across from Mrs. Gantke, corner Friedrich-Karlstrasse and alley.—

This letter is richer in things "concrete" and poorer in things "abstract" than my letters usually are. Sometime there will again be one of the other kind; in part, I'm lacking the necessary repose for that—you'll understand, I'm sure. Enclosed is a letter for "Püppi from Pappi." I'm happy that you are both comfortable in your new home. That it may remain that way, hopes—with heartfelt regard for you and the "little monster"—

TRUDE

38

Berlin, June 2, 1941

Dear Hilde,

How nice that Sabine is "frölich and glüglich" [cheerful and happy]— she looks it in the picture—hopefully she will one day also be "fröh- lich" and "glücklich" when she is not only, as she is now, "gros" [big] but really "groß." Cheerful and happy—it matters less to spell it right than to really be it. What nice cards children would write if they were not supervised in this activity by parents and educators so that what might be fun is turned into some sort of unpleasant school work through admonishing and carping.

The unpleasantness often comes not from preventing and eradicat- ing of spelling errors but from good advice concerning style and con- tents. (One never starts with "best regards"; that comes at the end, or "you haven't said anything about your doll; you should do that too" and "what will grandma say when you write only four lines on the big sheet of paper"? And the poor child finally "squeezes out"—under con- siderable pressure—a longer epistle to grandma and in the future will have little to do with writing paper or postcards.) It is similar with essay writing in school; I mean the home assignment. In Peine, one mother was irate that I let her little girl report only as much about her rabbit as she knew and wanted to tell, so that two lines were left blank at the bottom of the page. "How will this look? For those few lines she could have found one or two more sentences. And if she cannot think of anything right away then one just has to help her along!" The girl actually managed—with some "pushing"—to produce two more sen- tences. But I felt from her lack of enthusiasm that they were too much. . . .

From your letter, I see that you feel differently than I do when you say that everything about your former life "though present as a memory, is yet something completed and distant." I, for my part, feel closeness only between myself and that which once was. That which is happening to me now is for me unreal, remote. I may not be actually dreaming, but I'm also not fully awake. It is as if I'm wandering in a world of in-between, a world that has no part of me and in which I have no part. One of my acquaintances remarked during a visit last year that I said "at home" when I spoke of Finkenkrug, as if here in Berlin was not being at home for me. I was myself quite unconscious of the fact that I spoke that way; that I felt it, I knew. . . . Excuse the repetition in case I told you this little detail before. At any rate, as I wrote you several times since we've been living here, I've have been pulled from my soil by the roots. And what I yearn for is a soil where I can again take root. . . . What saddens and disturbs me about many letters from abroad, be they handwritten or printed in newspapers, is the fact that the writers lead a life sort of "up in the air" [*Luftleben*], that they straggle about rootlessly, and I'm not only speaking of those whose outward circumstances are not yet settled. No, also the successful ones, those for whom everything has fallen into place and those who, after some initial slipping on the steep slope, have climbed to the top of a secure existence. And even those who are working a plot of land and call it their own—what ties them to their piece of earth is a superficial link of providing and gaining sustenance, but the inner connection is as yet lacking. How could it be otherwise? One does not become within a span of three years a Chilean or Brazilian, no matter how well one speaks the language or how well one is situated, let alone in three months. Even though there are those who erroneously insist that they are able to pull off this trick. (I once read in the community newsletter a letter from someone who had immigrated to South Africa the year before—that is, before '39—that was tuned to the note "We South Africans.") This rootlessness is most apparent in reports from Shanghai, which seems, at least in part, a town where the foreigners live in what is exclusively a city of strangers. Whether a new native generation will grow in the soil where their parents are still strangers? I don't know. . . .

The old doctor's widow died in the hospital after all. The son, who was her only child, is deeply, very deeply affected by the loss, for besides her, as he says, he really doesn't have a single person in the world who is close to him. . . . And our communal living arrangement, which promised to be pleasant, is now in question. Maybe it will continue, maybe not. . . .

Thank you for your letter and also for the recent card for me, and best regards to you both,

TRUDE

39

Berlin, June 28, 1941

My dear Monster!

You sent me such a beautiful letter, so I want to answer right away. Can you read this? You write about the lake—on hot days like these, I too would like to be at a lake again. Do you still remember the little pond in Finkenkrug? Probably not. When I was a child of eleven or twelve, I often went to a lake; it was in the park of the castle Charlottenburg and was called Koch Lake. Why it was called that I don't now; it had nothing to do with cooking. There was a bathing pool with two attendants, Miss Lenchen and Miss Hedwig. They always wore enormous straw hats with enormous bows, and they taught the children to swim. They tied a belt around us with a long rope attached; then we had to jump into the water right away, and the attendant held on to the rope so we wouldn't go under. There were also rewards, just as in school. If one swam for half an hour without stopping, one was permitted to sew a silver ribbon to the bathing suit, diagonally across the chest. Those who swam for one hour received a golden ribbon. There often was a mother with six or seven children, who all stayed at the pool all afternoon. One was still in diapers, lying in the carriage, and the carriage stood on a wooden bridge which passed over the lake. From time to time, the mother left the water and gave the baby a bottle. One of the children was called Dorchen. Dorchen was only four years old, but she was already a very good swimmer. She was especially good in the diving-for-plates contest. Do you know what this is? It went like this—someone tossed a big pile of plates into the lake, and the swimmers had to dive for them, bring them up from the muddy lake floor, and hand them in at the edge of the water. Whoever brought the most plates was declared to be the best diver and received a prize. Sometimes it took a very, very long time for all the plates to be found at the bottom of the lake.

Once I had a funny experience: I was lying belly up on the water and didn't move at all. And slowly I went under and sank and sank until I reached the bottom of the lake. By then I had swallowed enough water, so I pushed with my foot against a stone and rose to the top again. That was right next to the railing of the bridge, and on the bridge were many people who looked at me surprised. What had happened was that a child had seen me going under and thought I was drowning and called on people to save me. The people came to pull me from the water and were now very surprised to find that I had come back all by myself.

Now I could still tell you the story of a big girl, who was heavy and strong, who jumped off the wooden tower and broke off the diving board and who crashed into the water together with the board—but I want to stop; otherwise, we'll have a flood from all that water. I wonder if I could still dive off the tower into the water today? I would like to try it again all too much. . . .

Yesterday I received a letter from your Mutti, dated June 23. I hope to have a chance to answer her sometime soon and send regards from the heart to her meanwhile. Also for you many loving greetings from

AUNT TRUDE

When Helene comes back—she's not with us right now but maybe in a week—I'll ask her for the recipe of the rhubarb soup.

40

Berlin, July 22, 1941

Dear Hilde,

Right at this moment, I'm sitting on the horn of a dilemma, of whether I should make coffee or go out (with Helene) to the mangle. But I do want to start this letter. First of all, I want to thank you for your letter, the one with the report of Bienelein's illness, the other of the seventeenth of this month, which arrived promptly today. And if

Sabine was cheerful despite everything [*drosdem lustieg*], we are happy to hear that she's all well again and can play in the "bear meadow."

And now once more thanks for your letter of the twenty-second of last month, which I can answer only today. Your ability to describe landscapes, moods, together with the inability to create a dramatic action with the "inevitable people" is nothing that unusual—it's something I understand quite well. You use the expression "to add some action to it." But you really shouldn't do that. The truly creative spirit, the genuine poet, doesn't do that. He doesn't resemble the painter who first paints a landscape and then, because he thinks the thing needs a lively touch, places some "strapping boy" or a "sweet girl" into the mountain surroundings or the familiar shepherd with his knitting yarn into a blooming heath. (Of course, I don't mean to say that all painters work that way; the great ones of their guild I'm sure don't do that.) No, he works more like the baker: action, landscape, mood, characters are placed into a bowl simultaneously and are kneaded together into a firm dough; once it is in the oven, it may be garnished or covered with a glaze afterward, or the burned spots can be scraped off, but essential ingredients can no longer be added. This is a method in which, for example, Busch excels; in *Max and Moritz* or *Schnurrdibur,* picture and word are inseparable so that reading and looking taken together give the impression of simultaneous creation, and it is not, as with other humorists, noticeable that the picture—or word—came first and the other followed as an explanation or illustration.

I'm well aware that certain writers, even some who have been dubbed "poets" by the critics, are basically in the same position as you are. Only you know the limits of your abilities, and they don't. I'm thinking of [Hermann] Löns. His landscapes and animals deserve, on a number scale, a "one plus," his human figures and actions barely a "five." And then there is the vast army of those who once wrote a readable book of youthful remembrances. With this, they exhausted their entire talent; they said everything they had to say, and yet, they continue to write. They write under different titles, in different forms, the first book over and over. Hermann Hesse, in my opinion, rarely rose above *Peter Camenzind,* and he repeated this book—with few alterations—several times over. See also Ludwig Finck, Otto Ernst, and so on and so on. Others of spritely mind and great technical ability but little creative imagination throw themselves into descriptions of lives and thus emerge all those many biographical novels we have nowadays. After reading your "Greek Travels," I'm convinced that you could earn your niche among the above-mentioned writers (I don't mean the just mentioned biographers but the others of whom I spoke down below on the reverse side), but fortunately your ambition probably does not extend that far. . . .

Excuse this long literary discourse—"well that too has to be sometimes." I should add that I don't count myself by any means among the select whose creativity pours forth like an inexhaustible stream. My river bed too dries up and not infrequently; but I don't plague myself with filling it with artificial canal water; rather I wait quietly for the rains from the heavens to renew the desiccated flood. Meanwhile, I neither write down my remembrances of Ebermergen nor another Robespierre biography, although I have plenty of material to bring to both.

I don't get around to reading very much now, and I have a strange relation with books in general. I'm living lately in a sort of—how shall I call it?—twilight of the gods [Götterdämmerung]; names of poets who were familiar and important to me from school or home are placed on a scale through their work and—found too light. Sometimes it seems to me that I have outgrown this or that book that used to fit me like a dress. . . . You are not angry with me that this letter contains so little that is personal? Some other time, I'll write of other things again.

Regards from Lenchen and Peter. From me, many of the very best wishes for you and the little monster

Your sister,

TRUDE

The proposed photo would really be the most suitable present together with a nice letter for Opa from Bienelein.

41

July 23, 1941

Dear Hilde,

Here I'm back again once more—at 4:30 in the morning. I must confess that I don't like my letter from yesterday much now that it is written. Not that I want to change my views or that I consider my remarks as wrong. I will mail it; but . . . it contains too little that is human. Only literature. It was actually only meant to serve as a beginning, an introduction, and then it was as if it turned into a rolling ball of yarn that kept on unraveling. And yet, I didn't write the letter in one fell swoop. Quite to the contrary, I was again and again interrupted by housework, and it was pretty much pieced together. I was constantly "torn out of it" and had to "get back into it" with each new beginning. Maybe you don't even notice it. But it would be disturbing to me to send you a letter that seemed to come less from the heart than my previous ones. Maybe what I dislike so much is also (for I have certainly spoken about poets and poetry often enough before) that it dealt with these things not in a manner of a mere connoisseur but, against my usual habit, of an expert insider. This is not usually my way, and I always withdraw when the conversation turns to literary discussions. I'm a poet; yes, I know that; but a writer [*Schriftsteller*] I would never want to be. The man who is a friend of Mary L. recently sent one of her letters to Vati. In this letter, she talks, among other things, about the completion of her Catherine the Great biography. She says she wrote the conclusion while the beginning was already being set into type. I cannot say that a book that is produced in such a way isn't worth anything, for I don't know it. But I'm a bit skeptical about what I would call a lack of respect for one's own work. Not to have it all together after the last line is drawn, as a whole, even if only for a short time, to read it as a whole one more time from beginning to end before the publisher receives it! I don't even ask that it be left sitting for weeks or months, which to my mind is doing a manuscript justice and which is something I afford mine. But what she says . . . that, as the work progressed, she delivered the completed pages to the printer and let the others follow . . . that smacks to me of factory work . . . of assembly line . . .

I don't want to say anything negative about either her or her accomplishments. She is, one hears it repeatedly, an unusual woman. And the way she works, her work tempo—I cannot measure up to. But there is something disturbing, something alien to me. . . . She creates for the moment; I try, probably with inadequate strength, to create for eternity. She is successful and I—well, it is not sufficiently important to me; that which is essential for me lies elsewhere.

Again heartfelt greetings,

TRUDE

42

September 3, 1941

Dear Hilde,

Thank you for the card dated the twenty-fourth of last month. Just imagine, on the morning of the twenty-eighth, we had a surprise visit from Suse. I was happy to see her even though this could happen only in the evenings. She returned home on Sunday.—Uncle Max and Aunt Grete wrote; they think that letters to you must have gotten lost since they haven't heard from you for a long time. They do send regards, as does

TRUDE

43

Berlin, September 21, 1941

Dear Hilde,

You can recognize my "sisterly affection" for you and the pleasure I derived from your letter by the fact that I "already" got up at seven o'clock to start this letter before I dressed despite the fact that it is Sunday, and I could stay in bed. The "already" is in quotation marks because this time is, for my current circumstances, late enough. On other days, I always crawl out of the feathers exactly three hours earlier. I really needn't do that and could sleep until 4:30, but there are always all kinds of things to be done before I leave the house, things I'm too tired to do when I get back home—polishing shoes, fixing sandwiches, and most of all, darning my stockings, which are, day after day, inflicted with new little holes. In the evenings too, there is usually some sewing to be done in addition to various domestic chores—reading, just sitting and thinking (or, if you want, dreaming), I don't get to do anymore, of course, not only because of lack of time. (Quite often after going to bed about ten o'clock, I promise myself to lie awake and meditate, but as soon as I pull the covers over me, I'm gone every time!) Since my bed has been set up in the dining room, I really no longer have an "abode," no space of my own, and the feeling of homelessness which I have always had here has now become even stronger. That the tenants, by their own testimony, feel quite at home here, is certainly nice. But as a result, there is this constant coming and going, also in our room; at least that's the way it seems to me. For example, when the mother brings something to eat for us, she often also sits down at the table to chat with Vati. Then the daughter joins us as well, and, with the remark that food tastes better in company, she settles down in a friendly way. And, of course, I cannot say that I have had enough company during the day and that a little peace and quiet and solitude would do me good. There are certain human beings who radiate an aura of peace and quiet; these people are, at any rate, not among them. They are outright social animals, and their good traits, of which they have many, are also of a gregarious, social nature. That's why, unlike myself, they loved and enjoyed the "good old days," and especially the daughter, who was, in her own opinion, the queen of the ball, was and is the most elegant woman, the best singer, elocutionist, sportswoman, preparer of fine foods one can think of, and whatever else. Her favorite topic of conversation turns on past festivities and the triumphs she reaped as a matter of course. She thinks I'm "strange" because her way of thinking and that of her world, which is the only way for her, is not my way of thinking, and since she has, in the words of Helene, a "little big mouth," she has told me this much to my face. In all this, it is admirable with what ease these people adjust to the present situation, which should depress them more than me. I already praised their great complacence, and for Vati, it is nice that he can tell them for hours his stories about his youthful and professional experiences. They love to listen, and he forgets, while talking, his pains.

During such conversations, I usually feel quite out of place, and not only because I already know Vati's stories, and not only when he holds forth. The conversations of the tenants too strike me as somehow alien. Since I'm away all day, I have practically "lived myself away" from home, in a manner of speaking. I feel a little what I sensed in the soldiers of the last war who returned from the front: they and those who had remained at home—without noticing—no longer understood each other; they spoke a different language. And even mutual goodwill to be closer cannot change this. Maybe it is similar among those who stayed behind and those who emigrated. . . .

About Sabine: I wonder whether other children at a certain age are more willing to help. From a certain age on, that is, when they begin, even if only in play, to lead their own life, the mother's demands for help disturbs their circles. I can say little about myself. I was of little use due to my lack of talent for the practical. About you, I know that when you had grown some, between twelve and fifteen, you were unwilling to lend a helping hand. I remember that when Mutti gave me this or that chore to do and I said I had already given it to you, she would only say: "Oh, Hildchen, she is not in the mood for that. . . ." You won't hold it against me if I confess that I was not very pleased with that—it did not leave any resentment in me, and I'm only telling you this so that you will regard the little monster's "egotism" with a little more forbearance. Margot, by the way, did, even as child, only what she felt like doing, and Mutti didn't even dare approach her with demands for help. One more thing: I believe that children display very early this or that negative trait; only most parents don't recognize it, and you do. The idea that adorable children can develop into unpleasant adults is erroneous: an educator with a sharp eye detects in the "adorable" child the little seeds of all the flaws that later thrive and grow wild and make it completely unbearable. You needn't worry about Sabine on that score. But it can do no harm, as much as you can, to imperceptibly nip in the bud the shoots in her character—better than having to pull the weeds later on. Mrs. Schmoller told me when she was a young mother, she was often reprimanded by relatives because she was, in their opinion, too strict with her children. She said she wanted to be able to afford treating them mildly later on. A reprimand for a four-year-old saves a well-deserved thrashing of the ten-year-old. You yourself started early with Sabine, and if all adults who meet her now take a liking to her, it is probably in no small measure due to the way you raised her.

I can well empathize with your "flower experience." I regret that I had so little of the beautiful flowers Vati received as a present. I had so little of it because I'm constantly out of the house. Now, they have long wilted. . . .

I passed on the greeting in remembrance of the twentieth. Helene received your letter for her birthday. Just now begins our New Year. That it may bring you and the child all the very, very best wishes, with a loving heart,

YOUR SISTER TRUDE

44

October 5, 1941

Dear Hilde,

Thank you very much for your cards of the twenty-first and twenty-sixth of last month. I was very happy to hear what you said about my letter. How much I would like to write to you more often, if I only had the time. You are, frankly speaking, the only person with whom my relationship has not flattened since the emigration; it has not only endured but has considerably deepened. I don't know Leslie's book. As you can well imagine, I get to read very little now and not at all to reading anything coherent. I borrowed Rilke's *Stundenbuch* [*Book of Hours*] from friends, and I look into it in the morning on the train, while I'm still half dozing, or in the evening before I fall asleep. Maybe I can read sometime something that is not already familiar to me (as long as it isn't poetry) but an unknown narrative, one that requires more and concentrated attentiveness, which I'm denied. Margot's birthday letter did not, or not yet, arrive; we did receive birthday letters first from Lindenheims and Uncle Siege as well as a letter from the Junge, written on Mutti's birthday. Thea's brother-in-law paid us a brief visit this week. The letter from Uncle Max is for the moment misplaced; that's why it is best if you use the address of Lindenheims who live only a few houses away from him: Montevideo (Uruguay), Avenida al Peñarol, 4290.

Best regards to you and the "diligent knitter"—I wish I had been able to do this as well as she when I was in school—from Vati and

TRUDE

45

Berlin, October 23, 1941
Four o'clock in the morning

Dear Hilde,

Your card from Z., dated the fifteenth of this month, arrived last night, and before then, we had two cards from Ascona and one of September 26 from Z. And then your letter which accompanies me on every train ride . . . Thank you! I wanted to repay you right away last Sunday; it was impossible for lack of time, and this coming Sunday, it's Sabine's turn. . . . You say that you can't help me as much as you would like— your letter alone is a great help! . . . And help also comes from another direction—from all directions—at least for me. . . . Good friends have lent me [Rilke's] *Stundenbuch;* I glance through it, still drowsy, in the morning on the train, and that too is a form of help. . . . We have now again the kind of "suffering of that great suffering from which man fell to small sorrow." . . . and for me (even if perhaps only for me), it is good to feel this. . . . (Did I write you all this already? Then please excuse the redundancy. What I know I haven't written.) Help was of- fered to me also recently through a small, brief interlude. I was sitting in our locker room (for about a quarter hour) alone on a bench with a young Gypsy woman; her face did not have the sharply drawn Gypsy features with the restless, sparkling eyes. Her features were soft, more Slavic; she was also relatively light. . . . And her face did not only have a sultry, submissive expression as in animals, as in old draft horses, cer- tainly that too, but more still, it had an impenetrable secludedness, a stillness, a distance, which no words, no look from the outside world could reach anymore. . . . And I recognized: This was it; this was what I always wanted to possess and did not yet possess completely; for if I had this, then nothing and nobody from outside could touch me. But

I'm already on my way to achieving that goal, and that makes me happy. . . . Vati's rheumatism is perhaps a little better, even if not much. . . . He is, of course, still asleep. Best regards!

TRUDE

46

[October 23, 1941]

My dear Monster, Bienelein, and Püppi!

Today I'm going to write in big letters and clearly in Latin letters so that you can read my letter all by yourself. This time my letter is not as nice as those that I usually send for your birthday—Aunt Trude would have liked to tell you this year also a long, beautiful story, if only she had time and leisure for it! But if one gets up every morning, except Sunday, at four o'clock and is away from home until evening! And on Sundays too, when one first gets a good sleep, there's much to do, sewing, darning, cleaning up, and writing letters which one doesn't get around to doing during the week—maybe it's the same with your Mutti; but she has a big girl by the name of Sabine who can help her! Today, while I have been rummaging around all day in boxes and suitcases, something funny happened to me.

We have here an attic that can only be reached with a ladder. I wanted to check out what was up there; I've never been up there since it's very difficult climb. Lenchen, who was visiting, steadied the ladder, and I climbed up. However, as I was aware, the ladder was much too short; I just reached the attic door with my head and shoulders. I opened it; the door has a rather high threshold. I grabbed it with both hands, and with a sort of pull-up, I swung myself up. And was up there—in an empty, little room with a low ceiling and even a window (usually these kinds of attics are dark). However, the assertion was not worth it; for I found nothing but a few boxes and our old, white children's bench and a few old lamp bulbs. So this wasn't anything, and now I wanted to get down again. Easier said then done. I sat down on the threshold and stretched my legs toward the ladder, but my feet didn't reach it; it was just too short, and its upper rung too low. If one has reached some height by pulling and swinging upward, and one wants to get down again, then one has to jump; but it is only possible to jump to the ground, a large space, not onto the narrow rung of a ladder. Maybe an acrobat at the circus can do that; I would have crashed. What to do? Lenchen suggested that I lie flat on stomach with my legs hanging down and then to slide down slowly until my feet touched the upper rung; this didn't work either. So I sat down up there in my little chamber and decided that I would have to stay and live, eat, and sleep up there for the time being; for I was unable to leave. But then Lenchen reminded me what Opa might say about this when he came back from his walk and found me up there; he would surely get very excited that I wasn't able to get down. So I made a last-ditch effort; I sat down on the threshold sideways, as if riding sidesaddle, and lo and behold, I managed to reach the upper rung with one dangling leg; then I pulled down the other leg and finally got down again.

This is the story for today; it's not long and beautiful and interesting like those I usually write you, and I haven't congratulated you yet either. I want to do that now and wish you and your Mutti all the best. I know my letter isn't as nice as I would have liked to write; but I want you to know that I love you and your Mutti very much.

Be well; I have to help Lenchen with folding the laundry.

Very best regards to both of you from your

AUNT TRUDE

P.S. We've been getting mail from the Junge recently.

47

October 26, 1941

[Letter to Susanne Jung; beginning is missing.] Believe me that whatever may come, I won't be unhappy or given to despair, because I know in my heart that I'm going the way for which I'm destined. . . . So many of us went that way through the centuries; why should I want to go a different one than they! . . . My father has lately been thinking of joining his brothers at the last moment (it is questionable that this is still possible at all); he wanted it for my sake since he regards his own life as already concluded—but I refused. Such a migration would be one that was merely imposed by exterior circumstance. I don't want to flee from what I know in my heart I must do. Until now I didn't know my inner strength and to know it makes me happy. [Ending is missing.]

48

November 9, 1941

Dear Hilde,

You cannot imagine what your letters mean to me, also the card of the twenty-ninth of last month, for which I thank you very much. To return to your last letter—it's already a long time ago—this elemental closeness to nature of yours is also mine. When I was passing the gardens of Lichtenberg during these autumn days in the evening in the streetcar, I was overcome by a strange feeling and became very nostalgic for F.—the people there I didn't love, but the meadows, the forest, and the "new plot of land" . . . And the animals, Flora! Oh, that I could brush and comb her just once more! Every time I meet the borzoi of the tenants above us in the stairwell, the wish rises within me. . . . Will I ever find this "lost paradise" again? I wrote you earlier that I moved to Berlin without any preconceived notions. But here, among these faceless, modern tenements "with every comfort" . . . Well, as I said, I already discussed this sufficiently before—I'm still sorry that my letter of the sixth didn't turn out the way I wanted it to be; but it just didn't go any other way. . . . I would love to write to you again sometime with leisure, and right now this is impossible. Do not repay me with the same; if you can, send again one of your beautiful, long letters to your sister

TRUDE

Vati sends best regards to both of you.

49

November 25, 1941

Hilde, dear sister,

Again a card instead of the letter I would have loved to write to you. But on weekdays this is impossible, and Sundays I don't always get up early enough, despite good intentions, so that I can write in peace and calm—it is the only day when I can sleep late. The course you are taking would have interested me too, very much so. I already have some knowledge in that area. I know that you easily get the feeling of being "superfluous," but you really shouldn't. I know it is essential and nice for us that our work has an effect on others; but then again it's not an absolute precondition of proof for the worth of our existence. . . . How else would I have to feel about myself, I, who doesn't have a Sabine, who has left the care for Vati for the most part to the tenants, and who engages in work at which I can very well be replaced any day? And yet I feel as if even the life I lead now has some meaning, as if I, as if it was alone in my hands to give meaning to the seemingly meaningless. In a story by Estaunié, a group of children on an excursion spot a few flowers on a rock that can only be reached through skillful climbing. A boy says indignantly: "Nobody can see these; what are they blooming for up here?" And the little sister answers: "So the world is made beautiful when the sun looks at it." That's my thinking as well. . . .

Vati's rheumatism is unfortunately not much better. He does not append a few words to this since he is, of course, now—five o'clock in the morning—still asleep, and I want to take this card with me. But I'm sure he sends you both his best, the same—with thanks for the card of November 14—from

YOUR TRUDE

50

December 8, 1941

My dear, good Hilde,

You don't know how very happy your card of the twenty-third of last month made me. Like all previous mail from you, I carry it with me always and read it again and again on the train. Yesterday, I paid a visit to Käthe. Your faithful thoughts apparently made her feel very good; she told me that she too thinks about you very, very often, and she hopes that the certainty that she is thinking of you may be, even if only in a modest way, for you a sort of staff and support to lean on, just as your thoughts are already of great help to her. She quoted Hermann Stehr: "We cannot help each other. Our greatest effort for the well-being of others consists in ceaseless striving for the best in our lives." Something to that effect. By the way, you may be doing her an injustice to admire her strength and endurance or even to ascribe to her such strength. For endurance is—as the word implies—something passive. But in her, there is something absolutely active: the belief in the capacity of man, even if not always and everywhere, through his own essence to transform an externally adverse fate, to wrestle with it, as Jacob wrestled with the angel: "I won't let you, lest you bless me."

I, myself, can understand such an attitude very well. I'm in a similar situation at my present work. I wonder if this makes any sense to you? More some other time. Today for both of you best wishes from the heart and with steadfast thoughts from

TRUDE

51

December 16, 1941

Dearest Hilde,

I wonder whether you will receive this letter in time for the twenty-seventh. It is questionable—but we wanted to wait for your letter to me, which has arrived meanwhile, before writing. And now it is here; I've already read it three or four times and each time with the same pleasure. Even if it is in your opinion, your own feeling, not as you wished it to be—your heartfelt, sisterly love is in it; it crept into the lines all by itself as you felt it inside of you. Did I ever quote a verse (by Victor Hugo, if I remember correctly) which I read on a French postcard in 1918 and memorized because I liked it so much? If you have heard it before, don't take it too badly—it keeps coming to my mind whenever somebody close to me apologizes for not having written a "beautiful" enough letter:

Pour écrire ce qu'on aime
Est-il besoin de tant d'esprit?
La plume va, court d'elle-même
Quand c'est le coeur qui la conduit.

[To write what one loves, does it need so much verve? The pen moves, rushes all by itself, When it is guided by the heart.]

And therefore I'll jump right into the middle of your own letter to let you know that I don't make fun of you at all for taking up sewing. On the contrary! I think it is something very good and useful. I think I should have taken such a course sometime myself—I didn't because I considered myself totally without talent in that area. But I wouldn't have had anything against making myself the clothes Wally made for me. I know that I often thought up—when I still had the time for such "dreaming"—garments I wanted to sew for myself—if only I had the skill! Wally, for her part, understood the mechanical aspects very well but had very little "sartorial imagination"; that is why whenever we tackled a project, we complemented each other quite well.

You bought yourself a Bible—and I own four! An old Luther Bible from the year 1854, it was given to Mutti's mother (according to the inscription); then I have the, though incomplete, Bible with pictures and marginal illustrations by Lilien; then the completely new, handy, thin-paper edition (without new testament), which cites Professor Torczyner, a Hebraist at the University of Jerusalem [*sic;* Hebrew University], as the responsible editor and which presumably also offers the most reliable German text. The translation is by various scholars; for example, the prophet Samuel was translated by Thea's father. Torczyner proofread everything and translated large parts himself and that which has its own rhythm in the original language has been presented by him for the first time as recognizable poetry, as hymn, also from the outside. This is also the reason why laymen and professional critics alike are very divided in their assessment of the new work. Thea's father, for example, was, of course, quite satisfied with his own work but did not approve of Torczyner's rhythmic texts. Mrs. Feld, on the other hand, whose father had originated the idea for a new complete translation, thought Torczyner's psalms and prophets beautiful but was not at all enthusiastic about the prose of the other contributors. She much preferred the Luther Bible, and even the later Zunz Bible. I, myself, reach again and again for the Torczyner, especially when I'm reading my Hebrew Bible—for I own this one as well—and need help with translating. I had been reading the Luther Bible all my life, and some people who are in a position to judge such things have claimed that its language has clearly influenced my poetic language. I remember a colleague at Döberitz saying once: "You talk like Martin Luther." Because I said: "This towel is dirty beyond all measure." I'm less well versed in the New Testament, and I have read, if at all, always only the Gospels; Paul and the other epistles rarely, and hardly at all the apostle stories. I would very much like to participate in your course. For even though, as I said, I know and honor the Bible, there is a good deal about its development that I could learn. . . .

How happy I would be had I an opportunity for a talk with the little monster. Even though I fear I'm not as good at it as I once was; after all, it's been years since I have "handled" a child. At any rate— where there is an innate talent—and I believe I have that when it comes to children—one doesn't lose it that easily, even if one is out of practice. I'm not surprised about what Sabine now reads. It was probably similar to the way she learned to speak. She lagged a little behind many other children, that's all.

And now you have waited long enough for a word about your birthday. What I hope for you is nothing more than what you wish for yourself—to find in the not too distant future, no, in the near future, a task that will fulfill you, that is more than just existence or a way of making a living. That it may give you a sense of "justification for living," which you, despite Sabine, don't seem to possess completely right now. And if there is something in you that can strengthen this feeling, then may it be the knowledge that you are a vital factor in your older sister's life—not very nicely put—that you are a tonic for her soul and that you fortify her inner strength. . . . Maybe this is too little for you, and I'm being selfish when I say that it is enough for me—

And now I want to close—I can't keep my eyes open anymore; I need to sleep awhile longer. This letter is not at all the way my birthday letter to you should be—not at all "beautiful." I wrote it in great haste yesterday morning between 4:30 and 5:30 A.M. and then this morning from 1:30 to 3:00. And, of course, it bears the mark of the way it was created. Nevertheless, I hope it will give you pleasure just as everything that comes from you gives me pleasure. . . .

Just a brief mention that a letter from the Junge to me arrived with only a slight delay for the tenth; I didn't get any mail from Thea, who had written just before, but from her brother-in-law, and yesterday came an airmail letter for me from Uncle Siege. None of these letters contained any "epochal news"; the writers are all well. . . .

Now I really have to stop; otherwise, I'll oversleep despite the alarm clock. For you and the child, greetings from the loving heart of

YOUR SISTER TRUDE

52

December 24, 1941

My dear Hilde,

I want to begin this letter today—but when end it? I have a few days' leisure ahead of me, and I want you to have some of that time since you have had to content yourself so often with postcards.

Thank you for your card of the eleventh. Opa is a bit sad that there's nothing he can do about fulfilling Sabine's Christmas wish for a doll carriage.

I read the three books (for sixty-five rappen); some I read before and some I owned. I found the Renan in the—long, long ago—the library in Arvedshöf, and he disappointed me. . . . But the *Portuguese Letters* I'm determined to read again soon, especially since I have now been stimulated by your letter; they are something eternal; this will remain so for as long as human beings breathe, men and women. . . .

And now, it's hard for me to find a transition to what I want to tell you. This is no great passion like that of the Portuguese nun; it fits more in a collection of "bittersweet love stories." Is it really a love story, not just bittersweet? I don't know. . . .

He, the hero of my story, is the "youngest and handsomest" among the workers at the factory. You see, how conventional a beginning this is; but I can't help it; he really is the handsomest and the youngest. Dark curls, tall, slender, sinewy, and physically strong, although he doesn't look it; a very pure, very handsome Jewish type, an intelligent face with evenly cut features, although their vivacious expressions often seem to blend over into a grimace. . . . I first noticed him actually only because of his quietness in the breakfast room. He was sitting alone, not at the general "men's" table. And when he was done eating, he would read. The first contact came through my knowledge of languages. Then, one afternoon, he saw me obviously struggling with a particular task; now that I have more practice, it is much easier for me. In a rather insistent and curt manner, he offered to do the job for me since his workday was already over. I refused at first, but he would not relent. It was hardly personal affection for me that prompted him to perform this act of neighborly love but rather an inner ethical principle. . . . But then, if I had been repulsive to him, he would hardly have thought of offering his help, and that this made him likeable in my eyes, you'll understand. A "reshuffling" in the breakfast room inadvertently brought us together at the same table. While we were eating, we frequently entered into conversation. But even before, when we were alone, he had started telling me very personal things about himself, honoring me, the stranger, with confidences that were quite unexpected, especially since he was usually so reticent. I expressed my astonishment. He declared himself absolutely certain of my trustworthiness for he had been observing me for a long time and then added a few things about me which actually testified to a rather astute faculty of observation. As things developed, neither he would pass by my workplace nor I his workshop without one of us stopping for a chat. In the course of this, I was amazed to discover many childish traits in him side by side with his unusual self-confidence and maturity. Then I found out that he was not in his midtwenties as I had believed, but just twenty-one, and I came to realize that he was still wet behind the ears. Actually, I now have the feeling that I took him for a bit too "old," too "grown-up," but I couldn't and wouldn't want to change that now. Maybe it was a mistake. . . .

This is how it was and remained between us for weeks. A few happy weeks? No, now that they are already memory, they appear to have been pleasant, but really content and happy I was not—neither with him nor with myself. Sure, I liked seeing him walk through the shop in the morning in his quite frayed, filthy blue linen suit, yet handsome and slender and strong and alive—I still keep that joy with me to this day—I was glad when he greeted me with a smile, yet . . . The "yet" has to do with the fact that our relationship seemed to remain where it was at the beginning; it did not develop, did not deepen, so that I never knew what name to give him. Anything that had the remotest connection with the little word "love" I could not and must not think of because of the age difference (but did he know how old I was?). Also he did not act in any way as if he did, and my appearance seemed unimportant to him. So was apparently my inner being. I often had the impression that he put great stock in what I thought of his problems but that he cared little for me. I was probably much too serious, too somber, too mature for him, and I noticed that he did not catch on to a lot of what I was alluding to. Too young for me . . . Had he been ten years older, we might have been a better match. But will he, in ten years' time, have fulfilled all the hopes that are now justly placed in him? He still has great, very great potential. . . . and he knows it too. . . . Anyway, I seemed for the most part only the vessel into which he could pour the overflow of his inner being. Can one speak of friendship in such a case? This too would not describe it exactly. And camaraderie? A camaraderie I could never have. I don't have the slightest talent for it where men are concerned; it is against my very nature. What was it then? Meanwhile, I discovered in him many character traits we had common. Counting the years, I could have been his mother, and occasionally, I thought: "My son . . ." Then I tried to act like a "maternal friend." It didn't work. It was he who made it impossible. He always treated me as if we were of the same age, the way he spoke, absolutely the "man," very sure, very determined, leading. And I did not dislike it. . . .

I didn't have to puzzle over all this for very long. For the end came—very suddenly, in a very strange way. Was it the new arrangement in the breakfast room that drove us from our table to blame at first? Maybe not even that . . . He had apparently been friendly before with a younger woman from the so-called second section. Now the tie between them seems to have become closer. . . . I don't really know her, just have seen her a few times. She is short, round, blond, neither elegant nor pretty; she has a fresh face with irregular, somewhat coarse features but makes a nice impression (maybe I tend to think the latter because I know he likes her). Most of all she is much younger than I, my guess is about thirty. On the train, I caught a few words of their conversation. They addressed each other in the familiar, but the whole tone was very friendly, not disquieting. . . . But . . .

The "but" concerns his changed attitude toward me. I noticed that for several days in a row he passed by my workplace without saying hello. Once when I went to his workshop to borrow a hammer I needed, he gave me short shrift. I've heard him speak this way to some of my female colleagues before but never to me. I didn't understand this sudden about-face and sought to question him. I asked him whether I had unknowingly done something that offended him. He denied it absolutely and honestly. He apologized for his harsh tone and blamed it on a cold and on being overworked. Not a word was true, but I had a pretty good picture after this conversation.

His attitude toward me since then has been most peculiar. When friends, colleagues, or companions separate without a quarrel, it usually happens through slow cooling, the friendship becomes tepid, loosens, and gradually the bond that holds them together dissolves; they drift apart. . . . An abrupt rift between friends only occurs after profound conflict, either hidden or open; an abrupt break without conflict occurs only between lovers.

This is how he acted, like someone newly engaged who turns away from a previous love, vehemently and decisively, who would even deny any relationship with the girl, in order to stand before his bride as an unwritten page. He now regards the whole thing as a mistake, would like to undo it if he only could, and he places a clearly recognizable latch before even the possibility of a continuation of the relationship. He doesn't say hello to me anymore; he doesn't speak with me anymore, and on those occasions when he finds himself near me, he looks intentionally past me. When we happen to meet in a "narrow alley" where we can't avoid looking at each other, he assumes a severe, defiant look forbidding me beforehand to open my mouth, to beg, to make demands, to insist on old rights. . . . And I?

Believe me, at first, his behavior did hurt and upset me. But then . . . then I was suddenly happy. . . . At last! here was the shot of the erotic, the drop of love I had been missing so totally from our relationship. It only entered into the picture afterward. For this is not how one treats a mere companion, a "motherly friend"; only a dismissed lover does one treat this way. He would be indignant, of course, and deny that this is what I was to him, and he wouldn't even be lying. Because he doesn't know it himself, and neither did I, had it not been for his behavior. A forty-seven-year-old woman still honored by a twenty-one-year old . . . instead of showing the old "grandmother" (I could be that by now too) indifferent respect as is customary among young people. I can't look at him anymore without smiling secretly: "Twist as you may, you still were once mine. What was between us was real, and try as you may you cannot undo it." And the labor of love I have been doing for him in our "good time," I'm doing still: after work I sweep his workshop for him. Will it remain this way? . . .

Enough. I wonder what you will say about this letter, which is so different from all my previous ones? Let me know soon. For both of you, very affectionate wishes for the new calendar year and greetings from

VATI AND TRUDE

53

January 1, 1942

Dear Hilde,

Your Christmas letter came on the day before yesterday. We very much enjoyed it and Sabine's epistle with pictures. You needn't go to the trouble of having them enlarged. Small photos are very nice and often truer to life than the others which often take on a strange quality in the enlargement. . . . The picture for me is really "monstrous" and just right for me. Today we also received a letter from Mrs. Spörri in which she tells us of her last visit and about Sabine, filling us with longing to see the "big girl" finally in the flesh! And you, of course, also. Judging from the picture, you have changed a little, which is hardly surprising after all these years. . . . The holidays were quiet around here. We received a letter from Thea after a longer pause (nothing new!). Helene baked something, and Margarete sent us a happy surprise. I just read Rilke's thirty-first letter from Muzot in which he expresses his happiness to have completed the *Duino Elegies*. I wish I could feel the same soon and report to you about it. . . . But it is not possible to force something like that nor can it be foreseen.—For the new year just beginning, the very best wishes for all things wonderful,

TRUDE

54

January 11, 1942

Dearest Hilde,

Now I must thank you for the card from the twenty-first and the letter to Vati and me of the twenty-seventh of last month, which arrived just yesterday. I can imagine Sabine's (and your) joy over the doll carriage; apropos of sledding, this makes me think of Finkenkrug and how I pulled her on the sled. Once upon a time . . . This not-letting-show very strong feelings, this rather-acting-than-talking is very typical of me also. Helene, whose tears flow easily, often says to me: "You are very tough. . . ." And I'm really not that at all. . . . By the way, she did receive your letter and card and will probably thank you personally some time.

As paradoxical as it may seem that we should have become closer through the spatial distance that separates us is likely due to the fact that all that had separated us in the past was only conditioned by time and place and was inconsequential and accidental, even though it seemed to us perhaps essential, and now the conditional, the accidental, has been stripped away. Chipped like the paint of a building that was not that important for its appearance in the first place. But the basic form remains unaltered. Thus, after the crumbling of the "separating coat of paint," what comes to light is that which unites, that which is permanent.

By the way, usually the reverse is true: the tie was knotted by accident, in passing; when all this disappears through physical separation, then the friendship disappears with it. That it may remain between us always the way it is now, wishes with best regards, also from Opa to both of you,

TRUDE

The letter made Vati very happy.

55

January 24, 1942

My dear little sister,

I just wrote a brief note to Leo for his birthday. I hope it'll get there in time. He is well, as are all our Breslau relatives. To you many thanks for the card of January 6 with the "pious Helene" (who happens to be visiting at the moment and sends regards). I just realize from the date of your card that I have left you without news from us for a long time; but I wanted to wait for the promised letter, which will presumably arrive as soon as I have mailed these greetings.

Nothing new from here—this is only meant as a sign telling you we are here and love you and the "little monster" very much. Now she finally has her doll carriage, and I guess for Hanukkah, she also received the little bed. Oh, it has been so long since I have played with a child, spoken with a child—sometimes I think I don't know how to anymore for lack of practice! When Sabine sees her Aunt Trude again, she may already have white hair—some of it is already here.

Vati is able to move his arms a little better, but it could all be much, much better. . . . He says hello to both of you. Likewise from the heart,

YOUR TRUDE

56

Berlin, February 1, 1942

My dear Hilde,

Actually, I wanted to send you a postcard as an "advance," but your last dear letter demands an answer I could not possibly give on a postcard. So I didn't get up too late today—you needn't think of sleep deprivation; it is already almost 8:30, but all the others here in the apartment are still asleep so that I have time to write to you.

And now, I feel as you do. There is so much I could tell you in person that is difficult to express in writing. At the very least, I must try, and I hope that I won't be too awkward, become incomprehensible, or create misunderstandings.

You see, my dear sister, here is something wherein we diverge from each other, not so much in thinking but in feeling. Had I not experienced what I did experience after all, I would probably agree with what you say about disappointment "lurking in the background," about illusions and reality. For many women, perhaps even for most sensitive women who are capable of strong emotions, what you say is probably true. But for me . . . Will you believe me when I say this: "I have never experienced disappointment," and "Reality was always unthinkably more beautiful than all illusion"? Will you believe me? This is how it was for me. It's not as if I have never been unhappy, as if I'd never suffered pain. No, I have been very, very unhappy; I have suffered great and profound pain, yet I loved it like an expectant mother is able to love the pangs of childbirth with which her child blesses her. But I always anticipated everything; I knew the great price I would have to pay. So there was no disappointment. I struck words like "forever," "constant," "faithful" (inasmuch as they should apply to my partner) from my vocabulary beforehand. This was probably all the more conditioned by the fact that I was never "the one," always "the other." . . . You might see me as undemanding; I was not. I had a low ignitability level and didn't catch fire easily—a fire that would extinguish quickly—but once it burned (how rarely!), then with strong and lasting passion. My feelings then had something of the quality of King Midas, who turned everything he touched with his hands into gold; it blossomed like a huge sun and gilded every spot, every pond, every puddle. And in the end, it was no longer important what he did, how he acted, he, to whom it owed its initial bursting forth, its warmth, its rays. The sun rises on the just and unjust. . . . you understand that I was never disappointed, never could be disappointed?

Not that everything I experienced or felt was always great and beautiful. I experienced much that was low, petty, and ugly, I had to wade through all kinds of morass. But afterward, I always told myself, and I still say it today: "What was, was good. . . ."

Dear Hilde, I would love to go on writing about this for hours more. But now, after breakfast, it is very noisy here; there is a "strange presence" that keeps me from continuing along the same lines as this morning (in between I had to search for a curtain cord for Vati). Maybe I'll take up spinning this thread again in another letter. Now, I just want to say that Opa and Aunt Trude very much enjoyed the description of the doll carriage. And Opa, of course, didn't know, until I translated it for him, what she meant when she said in Swiss German "How are you?"

The thing to "look through" must be a kaleidoscope. I remember, as a very young girl, Grandma Sch. took me to a department store. After we had done our shopping (I got all kinds of useful items), Grandma took me to the toy department and asked me to choose a toy. I picked a kaleidoscope—the mosaic pictures were created by turning a disc at the bottom rather than through shaking. One day, of course, it too did break; but I had it for a long time.

Again I'm not satisfied with this letter; it's a mere fragment, but I cannot let it sit until next Sunday since I will only then presumably be able to add what's missing. But you will take it as it is, won't you? And you won't be angry with me?

With loving greetings, also from Vati,

TRUDE

57

February 18, 1942

Dear Monster,

We received your Mutti's card of February 8 and the letter with your cards of February 11 and the card from both of you of February 12 and enjoyed especially your beautiful drawings. You sent me an owl; did your Mutti tell you that I love owls very much? I'm half owl myself because I can see very well in the dark. Only, I don't eat mice. I'm surprised that the mouse card for Opa arrived without the owl eating the mice along the way, leaving only the mushroom and the frog. Sometimes it also eats frogs when there is a shortage of food and nothing better can be found. When I was five and Aunt Margot was three, we got a little brother, and when Opa told us, "You have a little brother," I said, "I'd rather have a little owl." Your mommy, though she wasn't born then, probably knows this story. That was rather dumb, wasn't it?

But I was still very little then. Now I have written enough about owls, and I just want to send greetings for you and your mommy,

YOUR AUNT TRUDE

Are the hyacinths in bloom where you are? I love them very much too, especially the dark blue ones; they smell so good.

58

March 5, 1942

My dear little sister,

I felt the same way about your letter of February 7 as you did about mine. I wanted nothing more than to sit down immediately and answer it—there was so much I wanted to say to you in response. Today I happen to have a day off and can write to you in the afternoon, but something has placed itself "in the way" and is blocking the very thoughts your letter had stimulated and had only been waiting for ink and pen. This "in the way" are additional tenants. That is, the old-new tenant, Miss Meyer, the caretaker of the deceased doctor's widow, who lived with us once before. She is a friendly, good person, and I'm pleased that she came back. Then there is a gentleman who had been the tenant of other residents in the building. He seems considerate and obliging, and if that's how he really is, then everything will turn out fine. But, of course, this settling-in required a lot of changing the furniture around, emptying closets, hammering nails into the wall, and so on, and for an eighty-year-old man, the commotion was a bit much. At the moment, it is very difficult for him to get used to the new circumstances. But I'm hoping that in a few days everything will be back to the old routine, and he will have his order and quiet again. All the more since he is still alone all day here with Mrs. Fuchs. The rest of us leave very early in the morning and return from work only toward evening.

   For me, the whole thing was much easier. I'm just afraid that I may be disturbing Vati in his sleep in the morning (at least at first, eventually he may be sleeping through it) since his sleeping cove is separated from the room where my bed is only by a double curtain. There is a door frame, but the door was apparently never made and installed. I'm also sorry, though to a lesser degree, that for the same reason nothing will come of my writing "in the dead of night" for the time being, and I was always at my best writing very early! . . . But there is nothing anybody can do, and the letters which my heart prompts me to write will still be written somehow. Amazingly enough, I do manage, in spite of everything, and beside my work—to write.

A few months ago, I wouldn't have thought it possible under such strenuous physical demands: but, lo and behold, it works! Of course, it's "only" prose, not verse, a story; at any rate, this renewed creativity after a long hiatus is an unforeseen gift. The little work grows and thrives very slowly, but what does it matter; it grows and thrives, mostly in the morning while getting up and dressing and during the ride on the subway. The scribbling down on a piece of paper follows later during the morning break. And when I have advanced it once again by, unfortunately, only oh so small a step, and I think that what I did is good and beautiful, then I'm at times even quite happy. . . . For it seems to me, it must be true, genuine art that doesn't depend on hours of musing, nor on a desk and comfortable chair, nor the peace of a study and all that outward calm and comfort but is capable of triumphing over all those inauspicious circumstances of time and space. . . . A sign that here is not merely a small talent (that I knew anyway, but the confirmation of what I knew is nice) but that there is something deeply rooted, something that cannot be torn out, and despite all the cutting, all the trimming, it sprouts again and again and sends up its shoots.

Vati has already had his supper. I'm going to fix some soup now and prepare the sandwiches for tomorrow. I hope to continue this letter on Sunday. For now, good night! Good night to both of you, you and the little monster, whom Opa and Aunt Trude would love to see once more with their own eyes . . .

March 7

Though it isn't Sunday yet, but Saturday late afternoon; but who knows what obstacles to my writing will arise tomorrow, and so I want to begin again today. . . . You know—this just came to my mind—a book I recently found in the waiting room of my dentist (it's some-thing likely to be found only on a waiting room table) *Trotzkopf als Grossmutter.* I picked it up out of curiosity: unbearable. And then the wife of the dentist came in and gave one of the patients several serial volumes of *Berliner Rangen* to take home. . . . I turned again to the book I had brought along, the Babylonian heroic epic *Gilgamesh.* (Sabine, who once heard me say the name, said, "That's Wally's name" [Gillgash].)

The *Gilgamesh* epic is very close to me. I know, I feel that I come from the land where it originated, but I doubt that it would affect you in the same way. What I would like to recommend to you is another Insel volume in case you have a few rappen to spend: *Song of the Fa-thers* by Edzard Schaper. I saw it in a bookstore window several months ago. I liked the title so much that I thought to myself: "Either the work delivers what the title promises, then it must be wonderful, or it will be a disappointment, and in that case, I shall write a poem about Song of the Father; in order not to plagiarize, I can change the title af-terward." And it was wonderful, a discovery that made me happy. . . . And I think that you too would enjoy it if you knew it. . . . Later, I read a second story by the same author of whom I had known nothing before: *The Shipwrecked Ark*—also good but not unique, not close to eternity like the "Song." I believe he also wrote a larger work about Jesus. . . .

Second continuation. Sunday, early morning.

Actually, it is not that early anymore, already a quarter after nine; but Vati is not up yet, and I hope to finish this letter by the time he is shaved and dressed. Since I spoke last about books, I would like to re-turn once more to that little factory novel I told you about recently. As it turned out, the author decided to regard the end of the story only as temporary, as a transitory stage, maybe because he was not satisfied without a happy end and so let follow a sequel. The title is not bad; it consists of two joined-together quotations: "I Won't Let You Go, but Don't Greet Me Unter den Linden." The condition of hostile silence between hero and heroine continues in public as before. "Public" is al-ready the presence of a single third party, and when the woman comes to deliver an official message to the man in the presence of witnesses,

he looks at her as soon as she opens her mouth with a stern, almost angry expression, as if to say: "Don't dare start a private conversation
with me." And his face brightens visibly as soon as he hears something
like: "Why don't you look at Mrs. Langner's machine; the belt slipped
off again when she turned it on." But when the two meet while sweep-
ing the workshop, then it is he each time who enters—rather awkwardly though—into a conversation about trivial things such as: "So
for today we are done once again" or "If one lends one's tools to someone, they are certain to get damaged" and the like. The heroine mostly
leaves him to his little monologue at first and interrupts it only when
it gets to a more personal level; in the end, they usually have an exchange as in the "old days." Once at the streetcar stop in the afternoon—she rarely meets him there since he always leaves work later
than she does—he left his friends and joined her on the rear platform
but feigned complete surprise about this encounter. . . . Don't you
think that this whole affair is totally implausible and that the author
is a hack writer? A relationship as the one described is not unusual between lovers, especially in the case of a supervisor and a subordinate;
also between friends, something like this is possible. . . . but between
companions? . . . Something like this only happens in trashy novels,
not in real life. . . . Will there be a third sequel? I wouldn't put that
past the author either. . . .

So, and now I'd love to respond to various things you say in your
letter—and just now I must close. I would have liked to say a few
words about "stronger and weaker men" and about an "appropriate
type of work" for you—well next time. Sabine an archaeologist! What
won't she be as time goes on? I can imagine this to be very alluring to
a child: to dig around in the sand and to unearth some beautiful object, a real surprise. (Most children don't know anything about this;
otherwise many, especially boys, would want to become explorers of
antiquity—as long as the question of choice of profession is still in the
distant future. . . .) That she should be asking for the fire is really
amazing. . . . With best regards to both of you , also from Opa, who is
just visiting neighbors.

With much love,

TRUDE

59

March 27, 1942

My dear Monster!

May I still call you that? I used to say "little monster"; but some monsters are also big, and you are one of those since your mommy writes that you have grown monstrously. When Aunt Trude sees you again and wants to give you a hug, she'll have to use a ladder and lean it against you; otherwise, her arms won't reach your neck. I thank you and your Mami for the letter of March 4 and 16. I really wanted to answer right away, but unfortunately, I have very little time. You ask how I am; I'm doing fine. If you were here, you could already be outside a lot for it seems that winter is gone. How is your doll carriage? White? Or blue? Or green? And your doll? The Neumännchen?—I love to look again and again at the beautiful card from your Mami with the flowers and snake, and I'm always thinking of the two of you. Opa and I send you greetings from the heart,

AUNT TRUDE

60

April 6, 1942

Hilde, dear sister,

Your and Sabine's Easter greetings arrived on time, on Easter Sunday. I, for my part, must confess "to my shame" that I've been thinking of Pesach lately and not of Easter. As I did last year and the year before, I participated in a simple celebration of the former feast here in the building so that there is no mention of bunnies and eggs in my card, which the "monster" must have gotten in the last few days. This reminds me of a long Easter letter I once wrote to Wolfgang in which I told him that the specifically geographic variety of "Easter bunny" was not native to Chile, and the eggs were probably delivered by the condor. . . . How was the egg hunt this time in Zurich? The Easter bunny had probably already heard about the good report card and rewarded it with something special. . . . Or does the bird lay the eggs? From Margarete, who was so generous to us at Christmas, we have not heard anything at Easter, but since she told you that she would send us a present, a package may arrive any day. We heard from Leo only last week. He seems to be in a forward-looking mood, which is nice.

By the way, I didn't thank you yet for the "illumined" card. I like this one best of the three you have sent so far. The last, the spring card, is totally different from the first two. I can imagine that this picture is more appealing to a painter; "the distant world" and the "light" may even have some decorative value. I find their quality of the fantastic more stimulating than "ordinary" spring. I know, a poet should not judge a painting from a poet's point of view and that the static art of a painter has nothing to do with my dynamic, creative art, and yet— maybe it's this failed artistry and composition, this somewhat "absurd" quality, that attracts me, and also, you are right, it is reminiscent of my own poetry, especially *Welten.* . . .

With regard to the young man about whom you write in your letter of March 4:

It is nice that he senses about you an inner calm, and he may not be, despite everything, completely wrong in this. You speak of a certain maturity, which you do not deny about yourself; aren't maturity and inner calm closely related? Doesn't that which is mature have a core? And even though you feel in yourself a restlessness, the core is in you; but how many people nowadays lack this completely! I see it all around me: their character resembles a jellylike mass, colorless, transparent, reflecting every shade of the exterior events, without a firm center. And this, your core character (which I also address in my letters to you), is probably what the young man sensed and what he called "calm." . . . And he is, I said it before, not even wrong. You may seem to yourself disquieted, seem churned by storms like the sea; but somewhere inside of you is a firm island even if it is permanently washed over. . . .

I have in common with you a certain antipathy to friendships with women, but maybe it has, in my case, a different origin. Since reaching adulthood, I have had an irrepressible aversion to any kind of spiritual closeness with members of the same sex, an aversion as strong as what other women probably feel only about physical closeness with members of the same sex. Exceptions for me are relatives and childhood friends. I've never had occasion to discover this same tendency in other women; but I did observe such a spiritual "homophobia" (if the word doesn't exist, I'm inventing it) two or three times in younger men. That was in 1916–17 among soldiers for whom the constant, exclusive company of members of the same sex aroused an aversion against them, while for many other natures such circumstances usually led to the homoerotic.

April 7, very early in the morning

I have twenty minutes left and want to see what I can and want to write to you in this time. Oh yes, here it is: there's one area in which we are complete opposites—you said, although you are not ugly, your effect on men always derived not so much from you appearance than from your personality; the latter was, at any rate, primary. Will it surprise you to hear that in my case it was almost always the reverse? I'm—and was—surely not pretty and yet . . . Wherever I made an impression on men as *woman* (not as *person* besides all interaction between the sexes; this too happens frequently), it did not happen as one might think because of my personality, my spiritual being, but because of my face. Other women often had trouble understanding this. Ella once told me in Ebermergen that she once asked her husband during a train ride what was the effect I, though not pretty, occasionally seemed to have on men. And he, who found me by no means attractive, said it was my mouth and eyes. . . . It's funny, by the way, that the women in the factory generally assume that I must have been beautiful once and seem to think that in part one could still see it. Since I believe that I look at the moment rather haggard and worn and miserable and not very well at all, I thought at first that they were making fun of me. But then I overheard a conversation about me not meant for my ears and know that they actually mean it.

The whole thing makes me a little melancholy because in my old, "good" days, women always thought I was ugly. For many men, I was pretty, if no more. . . . maybe it's the other way around; it's hard to tell. . . .

Now I must conclude quickly. I'm looking forward to Sabine's "debut." What piece is it that she appears in? And what does the budgie look like? Is it naturally green or is it yellow and blue? Does it know any tricks?

For both of you greetings from the heart,

TRUDE

61

April 13, 1942

Dear little sister,

When I came home from work today, I found your spring card of Easter Sunday on my desk. We were happy to hear what you write about Sabine, especially that she likes to give her "all" when it comes to pleasing her mother. Hopefully, this will last a lifetime. What I wrote in my last letter about Margarete, that we had not received any mail of late, must be corrected. Meanwhile arrived Easter greetings from her, which made us very happy. And on the evening of our Pesach feast (April 1), I "finished" my little story—as we say in factory lingo. About twenty-six tightly written pages, in three months; that's a snail's pace, but I'm happy that it worked out at all. It seems to me this achievement is not only mentally but also physically invigorating. In any case, I'm of late, despite increased work, less tense in the evening than I have been. Hopefully, it will remain that way. I'm glad that Vati can be outdoors more now that the weather is warmer; it's good for him after all that sitting around inside during the winter.

From the way you mention Wöllishofen, it seems that now, with the coming of spring, you are a little homesick. I'm sorry about that. . . . sometimes I remember Finkenkrug. . . .

With best wishes from the two of us for the two of you,

TRUDE

62

April 27, 1942

Dear Hilde,

These few lines are meant for you and the little monster, because I received mail from both of you meanwhile: your letter, the flower meadow picture, and Bienelein's card. For now, many thanks. Your spring painting included in the letter made me homesick for Finkenkrug, for some plot of earth not covered with asphalt. . . . The description of the test, however, reminded me of Miss Schmidt's school in the Westend. On Miss Schmidt's birthday, we all came to class in our best dress, holding flower bouquets, and when we were in our seats, a huge bowl with colorful pieces of cake was passed around. . . . Sometimes we put on a performance for the parents who were invited. I remember a little conversation piece in French, "Les Fleurs." The children carried artificial flowers, which they were supposed to represent. I was "le nénuphare," the water lily. I always liked this flower very much, even in later years; it has something mysterious. . . . I hope to find time for a letter next Sunday. Until then, greetings from the heart for both of you,

TRUDE

63

May 2, 1942

My dear sister,

Your last letter—you must have received the thank-you card meanwhile—was until yesterday the only piece of spring I had to enjoy; the chestnut trees outside our window with their thin, little leaves make such a chilly, lost impression; maybe it only seems to me that way. . . . "Until yesterday," I said. For yesterday afternoon, I was stupid enough to get my finger caught in the machine; fortunately, I apparently got away with a flesh wound and a bruise. But according to regulations, I had to report to the accident station immediately. The closest station to us is in an insane asylum at the end of the street. (To say, "You're crazy," it is customary in our factory to say, "You got off the train two stops too soon.") The reddish yellow brick buildings of the institution are very beautifully located in a park with large lawns; in front of the administration building were rows of splendid, blooming forsythia bushes, and two broad-topped magnolia trees whose buds were about to burst open. . . . The pleasing sight did me such good, I forgot completely the intense pain in my finger and especially the very strong feeling of nausea. Meanwhile, I saw our house doctor, and I was glad he didn't declare me unfit to work; usually such injuries in our factory result in weeks of vacation. To tell the truth, I prefer the factory to being at home—this home which no longer is home to me. . . . For the alien, loathsome nature of our threesome tenants irritates me more and more every day, even though I control myself in their presence, the moral pretense of these self-serving, greedy people who constantly brag about their generosity and their feelings for others. The single tenant, who, like the others, belonged to Berlin W. W., is, of course, a close, good friend of theirs; but even my "only support," Miss Meyer, I have lost now. She is, as the saying goes, a good, dear soul but also an ivy growth, a winding plant that needs a stem, a staff to cling to. The stem provided for many years by the doctor's widow and her son, the judge; then, I guess, I served in that capacity for some time, and now the tenant Sch. has taken on that role. She helps him make sandwiches, brews his coffee, delights in his dumbest jokes, bends over laughing, for instance, when he pretends to be stuttering, and answers his casual, suggestive, or not so suggestive, talk in the same tone. She is neither young nor pretty, nor elegant, nor witty, and obviously he cares little for her, but her servile manner serves him well, and he rewards her with ironic, patronizing babble. Through him, she also made contact with the other tenants; good and decent person that she is, she asked me expressly if I took her new friendships amiss—since I make myself scarce as soon as the nightly "merrymaking of the populace" in the kitchen begins, she was visibly relieved and satisfied when I told her that I was not. She told me that she didn't like being alone and needed constant companionship, cheerful companionship, in order not to hanker after dark thoughts. . . . Vati too seems to have changed under the influence of our present environment and no longer seems to love his solitude. He moves a lot back and forth between our room and those of the others and constantly has to chat with somebody. With me too, while I'm writing this letter, which is not conducive to its growth, form, or contents. And yet, he's here for me "among larvae the only feeling breast," and we still have hours when we talk with each other the way we used to in Finkenkrug. Only these hours have become rarer. . . .

May 3, 1942

Now, about the factory. Actually, I'm now completely outside the circle of women workers. I'm not on bad terms with any of them; with some, I'm even on good terms. But I hardly ever join in their chatter. This desirable separateness is aided especially by my latest job at the machine. I work all by myself, independent of any coworkers, and only rarely need to talk with anybody if I don't want to. The only problem is that even now, as in the old days—presumably this is often the lot of quiet people—I'm regarded as a suitable receiver and keeper of confidences. There's especially a thirty-year-old psychopathic, half-Jewish woman who is obsessed with talking about her "gentleman" or "friend" and bores me to death with her stories. I rebuff her from time to time, but the effect of my rebuff doesn't last long. But then this woman is also especially obliging toward me, always ready, whenever I'm struggling with something, to come to my aid. She insists that I'm a very just person, even when I yell at her, and that's probably actually the case. Otherwise, her behavior is unpredictable; she is often recalcitrant and hard to handle. We have a few other psychopaths of both sexes who are just like her. These people, with whom normal people often have great trouble, do me all kinds of favors when I ask them and are very attached to me. I can't explain why. I remember though that in the old days I used to think sometimes: "If I were a man, I might have wanted to be a psychiatrist." I guess I do have a certain innate talent for dealing with such human beings.

My young companion, with whom I have spoken of such things on occasion, won't hear of it at all. He's by training a medical student and shows much sympathy for physical suffering, but he rejects any suggestion of mental illness. I can't really blame him. By the way, our relationship has meanwhile entered a new—fifth or sixth—phase; that is, it is better than it ever was in our best of times. But a burned child shies away from the fire; I don't trust this peace and doubt it will last.

Also, this relationship (I don't dare call this a friendship) is as far from making me completely happy as it was in the beginning. Although I'm no longer merely a "receptacle," there is something volatile in the spiritual-psychic aspect of this whole affair. Today we are getting a step closer; tomorrow it is being undone. It is not my fault; neither would I blame him, because I think I was like this too when I was his age and acted similarly. . . . How ever this may be, despite the latter consideration, when I'm at home, I always resolve to break with him, or less violently, to dissolve the bond. Now, it's I who no longer seeks him out, and he is the one who comes to my workplace. He has to come since it is part of his job to keep the machines in running order, and mine often acts up. As I see him standing before me, when his beautiful, intelligent face, covered with soot and often poorly shaven, lights up, when he says hello in the morning, then I just don't have the courage to say the parting word. But tomorrow, Monday, I'll do it, tomorrow for sure. Even though I remember how concerned he was when I had the accident, how he jumped up and made sure I got a sick note—but then he always shows concern, whenever somebody is involved in an accident. The day before, I even flushed a wayward, gleaming iron splinter from his eye with drops of water.

Tomorrow I'm going to take the opportunity to confront him about a minor matter I dislike about him. That will separate us, I think. I'm not the kind of female who reaches for sheaves of straw, and the thought of an older woman fishing for younger men goes against my grain. I would have liked a true friendship; but this unnatural condition of friendly closeness is in the long run too tormenting. . . . Strangely enough, like all men with whom I have been close, this one too is engaged. But then he is not that close to me. . . .

Dear Hilde, I must bore you with the never-ending sequels to one and the same romance. But nothing exciting ever happens here, and my experiences, as much as I dislike the fact, leave a stronger impression on me than they used to. My experiences gain in intensity what they lack in extensity. When I was in my twenties, and occasionally even later, I knew more than one man without having a desire to deepen the relationship. This last one is, of course, not the average, and maybe in the end destined for greatness, but is he also chosen? . . .

Otherwise, since I have distanced myself from the women, I have become much closer to our men. I believe I'm pretty much the only woman in the shop they take seriously and whom they don't dismiss with a snide remark when she wants to take part in a conversation. With two or three or even four of them, I'm on very good terms, especially the older colleague with whom I used to work the nightshift alone. We would perform whatever task was given, quietly and evenly. Hours would pass without a word that had nothing to do with the work. This being-silent-together, away from the chatter and gossip one hears all around, was so refreshing. . . .

Now, I must close. I'm going to read the letter over once more. I don't think I'll be pleased. I spent an eternity writing it, constant interruptions. You will take it the way it is, won't you? You will be content with my good intentions?

Today arrived your pretty card for Vati from the Fischstube at Zürichhorn. Many thanks. It is not at all summery here. On the contrary. When I leave in the morning, it's always only one or two degrees above zero. That Margarete has meanwhile reported to us in a "handy manner," I told you already. We will thank her personally and send our best wishes. Püppi's handwriting is getting better with each card. The last one is "picture perfect." For her a kiss. For both of you warmest greetings!

TRUDE

64

May 12, 1942

Dear Hilde,

Your card of the third of this month made us very happy. Vati was especially glad that you had heard from our dear ones, and I was perhaps equally glad about the narcissus from Tessin. I always look forward during my early ride (which is still ahead of me today) to the light green honeysuckle around the old Lichtenberg church, also a small, pink almond tree in front of an almost rural little house—near the old estate are still a number of surviving peasant cottages—and to a few blooming plum trees in the little garden. The trees are blooming late this year; their time is usually about the end of April.

Otherwise, I'm enjoying the *Duino Elegies,* and, to understand them better, I'm also rereading the *Letters from Muzot*. Do you know the elegies? In the ninth, for example, is the Roman rope maker and the pottery maker from the Nile of whom Rilke speaks in his letters. Your mention of baker master Weise reminded me of the wonderful crème baiser torte Mutti would sometimes order from him, and I felt the taste on my tongue. . . . May the joys be always greater for you than the assorted sorrows of which you speak. And the little monster must certainly be a great source of joy for you. . . . Little heart. Greetings to both of you,

TRUDE

65

May 19, 1942

Dearest sister,

Did you have the feeling yesterday in your sleep (for at 4:30 in the morning you were surely still asleep) that I was thinking of you with particular intensity? I was pulling on a pair of your old children's stockings for going to work. With these, I'm wearing a pair of good, but slightly too large, old-fashioned boots from Mutti. They don't make a very elegant appearance in the street, but they were nice and warm in winter. Now I will have to put together some other footwear. I cannot wear anything especially nice since there is a lot of wear and tear on shoes and stockings.

I just realized to my horror that I used up already half of this card without having written anything "reasonable." Many thanks for your card of May 12. I still like it even though Vati thinks that the wavy lines and bright colors make one dizzy. The "light" card for me is still, maybe not the most beautiful, but the most stimulating in the series. I can imagine the trees in Zurich in bloom around this time of the year. I'm always a little bit homesick, if one can call it that, for Finkenkrug. . . . Did you get Leo's letter? He asked me if you wrote anything about it to me. Vati is still asleep, therefore, greetings to both of you only from

TRUDE

66

May 20, 1942

Dear Hilde,

Of course I was happy to hear from Thea, even though Vati may have been more "overwhelmed." I presumed that, despite the long silence, she, practical and ingenious as she is, would find a way to feed herself and her child. Vati, by contrast, is always inclined to believe that when he doesn't hear from his loved ones that something is awry. And this thought bores itself into him and cannot be removed with reasoning, only with "hard facts."

Some other time, more of what's essential. Today only, again before going to work, for you and the "captivating" creature, greetings from the heart,

TRUDE

67

June 12, 1942

My dear Hilde,

Thank you for your card of the twenty-first of last month and the dear letter with Bienelein's zoo story and photographs. Opa will and wants to write to Bienelein himself. I wish I could answer your letter already the day after tomorrow, but if the weather is nice, I want to make a day excursion to the Westend. I'll be able to write in greater detail on another Sunday. And yet, when I first read your letters, I always feel the impulse to sit down immediately and write. . . . No, my finger is still not healed completely; this can take months, but it does not hurt anymore, neither does it handicap me in any way. Meanwhile, I was working for about ten days "with the men." The work is physically more demanding than my usual work, but there was such a wholesome, "heavenly peace" that I returned to my less strenuous activity with regret. Concerning Schaper: *The Song of the Fathers* is much more beautiful than *The Ark,* even though the latter is quite good; but the former is unique. . . .

Nothing new from us otherwise; only the "old and good" wishes for you two loved ones,

TRUDE

Today arrived your card of the seventh. Thanks.

68

June 23, 1942

Dear Hilde,

The promised letter is still not "rising"; again a postcard as an install-ment. Starting July 6, I will in all likelihood get a week's vacation; then I can write to you in leisure. Nothing new about us here. Some-times it is hard to imagine that we are already in midsummer. In the early morning, it's always still quite cool, and in the last weeks, we had a few days when it was outright cold. (I'm talking about the weather, which is the thing to do when one has nothing else to say. This is not the case with regard to you. On the contrary, I have enough to tell to fill whole pages, but it's not worth getting started on a postcard; it's only meant as a greeting and a "sign of life.") I believe Opa still owes Bienelein an answer to her zoo letter. It is more and more difficult for him—hardly surprising at his age—to get himself together and to sit down and write.

5:30 A.M. I still have my bed to make and my shoes to put on. Be very, very well, both of you and to a "more unhurried get-together in the course of the week after next!"

TRUDE

69

July 6, 1942

My dear little sister,

Still no letter from me, not even in answer to yours of the twenty-eighth of last month. Will you be angry with me? But the expected time off has still not "arisen." But I'm off today and tomorrow, but Suse is here since yesterday morning, and I'm spending as much time with her as I can. She sends warm regards. So again today only a "sign of life" . . .

Yes, this kind of drawers can be found at Aschbrenner but also everywhere else; I guess they lasted longest in decorators' shops; by the way, our Bolle keeps his noodles and barley also in a drawer—Yes, I went to the Westend—with beefsteak and potato salad in an old aluminum milk can from Thea. . . . I plan to go again next Sunday; but I'm plagued by a bad conscience since this outing means that you will have to wait awhile longer for the promised letter. But I'm sure you don't begrudge me the recreation, do you?—My fingernail has now fallen off, and a new one is already sprouting; it looks ugly, but I hope it will all soon be all right. I want to write to Sabine sometime about the "old days"—but when? Vati is still asleep. I'm greeting you both for him. With deepest affection,

TRUDE

70

July 19, 1942

Dear little sister!

Slept today to about eight o'clock, almost four hours longer than on workdays and in addition to that—for once at last!—blue skies and sunshine outside the windows. I should feel here, at Vati's desk, as if I was on summer vacation. If I still don't quite feel that way, but feel more like someone recovering from a long illness, it's the fault of the years into which I'm gradually moving; when I think about other women of my age, I must say the years are treating me still mildly. . . . It is now one year since I have been at work, and in that time, I never missed a day due to illness; I even managed my accident without taking time off. I believe I hold a record in this among all Aryan and Jewish workers, male and female, in our factory. (For the future, I cannot, of course, guarantee anything. . . .)

You say in your letter of the third of last month that your physical strength is diminishing more than it should. I'm sorry that you are not doing physically as well as I. My strength has definitely grown with the increased demands. When I think back to the beginning, when the woman's work in the factory was bitter and hard for me, and then to think today I'm working with the men in the men's section as an equal replacement for a few other men who were given notice because of inadequate performance. . . . Recently, I worked again for three, four days with the women, the work itself is quite relaxing—compared to the masculine activities—but all that chatter and screaming did get on my nerves. I was, therefore, glad when the men's supervisor appeared and declared that he couldn't do without me forever. Of the five people in our apartment who work in the factory, four are engaged in the same task day in and day out; only my work is more diverse. I started out like the others with a monotonous activity. What happened was that I soon began to regard the factory work not only as a bitter necessity, as coercion, but I began to see it as a kind of learning experience, and I wanted to learn as much as possible. . . . Yes, I even notice that I'm developing a feeling of being at home there, which I no longer have here, and I know that tomorrow, Monday morning, when I enter the slightly darkened halls, I will feel: "Home again." That's truly the way it is (I have written about this already): I have told my fate, "I won't let you, lest you bless me." And Schiller's words too fit me: "Gather the godhead into your will, and it will descend from its cosmic throne." Alas, alas, and this is what depresses me so, my viewpoint, my attitude, whenever it is expressed, almost never finds an echo. It is, therefore, only rarely openly expressed. I cannot impart any of the mental strength that I do possess to my companions in misfortune. Were I to become more deeply involved with them, they would only diminish my resolve without any gain for themselves. They do not understand me, think me perhaps presumptuous. . . . I cannot speak with them of the things I speak about to you. I'm sure it is nothing new to you that the years of the past, when everything in life seemed to be going "very well" for us, meant nothing to me. Our circumstances then required qualities mostly of the gregarious, social kind, which I lacked to a great extent. But the qualities required by the present time, I possess almost abundantly. I'm up to today's demands. When I was a child, I always wanted to be a Spartan; later I wanted to be at least a heroine. I urged Mutti to cook the black Spartan soup, and I loved our lentil soup because Vati thought it must have been the one the Spartans ate. One day, I put my hand into the open hearth to imitate Mucius Scaevola. Now, I no longer need to resort to simulation. I can, what was in my youth not even good etiquette, be an "original hero" (without standing out like a sore thumb). "What one longs for in youth, one has in old age in plenitude." That's why my attitude doesn't really deserve any admiration, at least not the one that is sometimes granted to a *virtue,* more one that gives *talent* its due.—Be well. As far as material to write about, I could go on for hours. But on Sundays, the housework tends to pile up, and especially today, I still have some washing to do. I won't forget a letter for Sabine—but when? I would like to repeat something you said: "I always think of you, even when I don't write."

Today writes and thinks even more of both of you,

TRUDE

71

August 4, 1942

Dear little sister,

I was, I almost want to say, touched that you wrote (on the twenty-sixth of last month) without any particular reason and only to "say a few words" to me. One evening, Püppi called me into her room: "Come!" "What do you want?" "I want to tell you nice words." She meant loving, caressing words. I'm thinking of this now. . . . Whether I already thanked you for your card of July 17, I don't even remember at the moment; at any rate, you should have received Vati's and my letter meanwhile. (Püppi would have laughed just now; I have a cup of malt coffee near me on my desk, and I was just about to dip the pen into it instead of into the ink pot.) Oh, how often I have the desire to write to you, but every time I'm particularly in the mood to do it, nothing comes of it. Lately, I've been getting back very late in the evening so tired that I even had to put off things like darning stockings until the next morning before going to work, so it never even

came to a "lousy" postcard for you. The entire Sunday too is spent doing housework. More about this some other time; also more about the
essentials.

I'm now approaching a stage at which I simply slough off anything
that is unimportant to me, and I distance myself mentally from it. . . .
But these are only greetings, however much from the heart of

YOUR SISTER TRUDE

72

August 8, 1942

My very dear sister,

Whether I begrudge you your vacation? The expression "begrudging"
has to be struck out altogether. I'm very happy for you that you have
the opportunity to relax—I wish I could do the same. However, it's
not so much wandering for which I'm in a mood—I run around more
than enough—no, what I would like is to sit somewhere in the sun for
hours, at a beach facing the sea at dawn or gazing out onto an expansive, perfectly still plain bordered in the far-off distance by gently rising, bluish hills. Maybe these are images of the Holy Land that rise before me. . . .

I'm happy that my letters are exactly what you wish to receive.
Yours, in whatever form, are always a soothing balm for me. . . . Your
understanding of my attitude, which you express in your letter of the
second, therefore, makes me feel good. Of course, it's possible that an
emigrant understands me better then those who have stayed behind,
since, by being outside, one gains a greater distance from all the events
than if one looks at them from the inside. Here, it is admittedly hard
for people to look beyond their own walls, their street, their part of
town, and my broader perspective arouses more astonishment than admiration. I notice on occasion that I'm dismissed as an "eccentric." My
attitude is only shared by my friends, the couple in Westend, and my
work companion. I have made repeated attempts to separate myself
from him and to establish the same type of relationship I have with
other coworkers. I didn't succeed. He's apparently determined not to

be cross with me no matter what I do or say, while with others, if they said or did the same, it would be grounds for a breach. "Just to see this man," a female coworker, who had been with us for only a short while, once said, "makes me feel like throwing up. This face, the way he struts through the halls, pure arrogance. . . ." And I enjoy what she calls arrogance, which may come from the actually somewhat haughty expression of someone whose fate may break him, but it cannot bend him. . . .

What you say about your diminished physical strength may be correct at the moment. I would hardly have thought years ago that I would hold up as well as I do under the strain of getting up at four in the morning and the daily exertion; apparently, it is as if my greater mental strength had carried along my weaker body, and it would probably be the same for you under similar circumstances. Unfortunately, much that is happening around me drains the mental fortitude I need to maintain so urgently; it's not the times, not the world, not the factory, but exactly that which should be a source of uplift and refreshment: the domestic life. . . . It's for this reason that I make sure that, whenever possible, I spend my days off outside our four pillars, and I often have mild disagreements with Vati that are better avoided but are often unavoidable. Although he too likes to visit neighbors and does so frequently, he thinks that my walks so far afield are too strenuous for me, and I had better stay home. Home—as if I still had such a thing! Aside from the fact that there's always some chore waiting for me here, which, when I'm not here, simply has to wait and that Mrs. F. likes to saddle me with all kinds of small tasks that are her responsibility—aside from all this, the whole place seems to have taken leave of all good senses since the new tenants moved in. All I see and hear is useless, unpleasant, and evil. Vati has been seized in the last few months by much restlessness and irritability, which I try hard, but in vain, to come to terms with; it is difficult for me to reestablish our old, close relationship, which, I must admit in the end, no longer exists. He has grown closer and closer to our tenants and to the level of our wider surroundings, and at the same time, he has grown ever more distant from me. His whole character seems changed. He expresses a keen interest in all kinds of rubbish and gossip and all kinds of stories about all kinds of people, something he always rebuffed in Finkenkrug more strongly than I, all of which is to me at best inconsequential. (And I'm only willing to concern myself with matters of importance, and everything else I toss off like a worn-out garment.) He listens with great pleasure and gullibility to the distorted, exaggerated stories which the young couple brings home from the workplace, about God and the entire human race. True, he asks me sometimes about my experiences, but since I have nothing to tell that is stimulating and exciting, he doesn't even notice when I fall silent after a few words. He really doesn't want to hear my answer and is not at all interested in what I have to say. . . . This state of affairs, of which I dearly wish it were different, makes me sad; it gives me a heavy heart, and I have only recently come to make every effort to follow the advice of my Westend friends. They seem to believe that this unpleasant behavior is part of advancing senility and that I had better begin to close myself off psychologically from the man he has become rather than try to live with him in harmony only to fail again and again. They tell me to remember him the way he once was and that I should not be sad about the way he appears now and accept conditions as they are with greater equanimity. He is over eighty years old and at that age has become much narrower, and not only the arteries. . . . True, but it pains me nevertheless. . . .

Today, as on other Saturdays, he was again in the morning in the synagogue. Not that he has become "pious" all of a sudden. First, he finds among the visitors an old acquaintance, and then he warms up memories of his youth; somehow he recaptures certain moods, echoes of childhood. . . . I understand this, and still it makes me uneasy to hear him talk about it like a "committed Jew." Coming from him, who was always free of religious bonds, sounds to me—excuse the expression but I can't find a better one—contrary to style.

Uncle Max once wrote a letter to Ilse in Paris in which there was much talk about the good Lord. Ilse was amused by it, but he said: "When she gets old, she'll turn religious too." I, for my part, don't put much stock in such late-life religiosity and wonder whether God likes it? After all, he is no beggar whom one can satisfy with leftovers, to whom one throws a bone to gnaw on like some leftover from a sumptuous meal, with the hope that he will be grateful and hand out the reward as if it had been a delicious, juicy roast. I can picture Ilse's face when her father exhorts her to pray. As if that were such an easy thing to do and merely a matter of good will . . . For modern man—in other times, it may have been different—nothing is probably more difficult than true prayer as distinct from mere repetition of formulas. Do you know when I prayed most fervently? Not when I was unhappy . . . I heard the deep breathing of the slumberer next to me at night. And I reached out with my hand without touching him, and I saw in the ceiling a blackish blue sky with singing golden stars. And I sat up in my bed, and I prayed. . . .

A few days ago, right after I had mailed my card to you, your greetings of July 29 arrived. You are asking me to write a brief note as often as possible. Well, yes, but brief cards are not really my style. For those to whom I have not much to say, I can get together a brief card. But for those, like you, to whom I have something to say, I much prefer to write long letters. I'm sure you would like to receive such a letter more often; but since it cannot be, I must, as much as I dislike it, comply with your request for at least a card. It always cramps my style when I can't spread out in writing. I'm like a fish that needs a large body of water, not a narrow container, to swim around in. Today I have been frolicking in a real lake. . . .

Together with the letter from you came dear pencil scratchings from Amden to which I will soon—tomorrow morning, I hope—respond. "How is Helene?" one reads there. Unfortunately, not good. A few weeks ago, she fell in the street and broke her thigh. She's in the hospital. I asked Else to let me know how she is doing but haven't heard anything yet. This sort of thing is very painful, and it doesn't heal very quickly, especially in somebody at an advanced age. According to the first news from the niece, even in her hospital bed, she worried about the laundry that was just to be done; she was on her way here to do it when the accident occurred. I immediately wrote her a letter to set her mind at ease and told her that I had washed most essential things myself, and that it had turned out quite well. The good soul . . .

A week ago, I started reading *Malte Laurids Brigge.* I'd like to discuss several points with you about it when I'm done with it. The book seems to me Rilke, and yet, not only Rilke. . . . I don't know the novel *Perpetua.* I'd like to read it sometime. Is it by Wilhelm von Scholz, or am I thoroughly confused? Then excuse my mistake. Thank you for copying those words for me. I'm sure you are right; what they say about the two of us is beautiful and apt. "Your sister lives apparently removed from life. . . ." Yes, yesterday on the train, a strange sensation came over me: I felt as if all the chatter, the commotion, the mass of humanity had become so remote from me, it was as if I had died and was beyond all of them, beyond their petty quotidian concerns, beyond any sense of community with them. Such peace was in me, a deep abiding stillness . . .

And now be well. I spent almost the whole day writing this letter, and the washing and sewing and cleaning just had to wait. But is the one not more important than the other? In a moment, it will strike eight, and I must think about Vati's supper.

I hold your hand in mine,

Your sister

TRUDE

August 10 (5:30 in the morning)

Yesterday came your card from Küßnacht—thank you very much. At the same time, news from Helene. The poor dear has to guard the bed for six weeks before she'll be x-rayed. The pain has fortunately lessened, and yet . . . I feel sorry for her.

73

August 10, 1942

My dear Monster,

Opa and I really enjoyed your card. We are both fine, but Helene unfortunately fell in the street and hurt her leg very badly, and she must stay in bed. It is wonderful that you are going on such a nice summer trip. When we were children, we always spent our vacation with Opa and Oma at the seaside. We went out with shovels and buckets and dug around in the white sand. We collected seashells and caught jellyfish and sometimes little crabs. And, of course, we spent a lot of time bathing. I think your Mutti was still very small then and may not remember anything about it. Be well. With best greetings from Opa and

AUNT TRUDE

74

August 25–29, 1942

My dear Monster,

I hope you received the card I sent to you to Amden. Yesterday, we received a letter from your mama; she said you came home chubby and tanned (the card was dated the seventeenth). We are happy, Opa and I, that the trip did you good. It's now between five and six o'clock in the morning, and I don't have much time left to write. But I want to start this letter anyhow because I'm just thinking of all kinds of things I want to tell you about.

My tenant, Mrs. Berg, told us last evening about her childhood, her toys, and a big iron doll cooking stove with polished aluminum pots and pans. She told us about her little brother, who once cut up an apple into little pieces, dusted them with chocolate powder, and cooked them in milk. It was apparently a ghastly grub, but the children ate it anyway and pretended that it tasted wonderful.—Well, we too had such a doll cooking stove, but we almost never cooked on it; the stove had to be heated with petroleum, and your Oma was afraid that we might spill some and that we would have a fire. We played mostly with our dolls. My doll had brown hair and blue eyes, and when it was new, she had a pink silk dress and her name was Elizabeth. Aunt Margot's had blond hair and brown eyes, wore a burgundy silk dress, and was named Frieda. Your mommy's doll was Gretchen, I believe. There was one doll with very short blond curls I named Helene; her little dress looked like a ladybug, yellow red with black dots. We also had all kinds of stuffed animals. I had a very pretty little brown dachshund. But all these toys were not as important for us as they would be for children who live in a city apartment, for what we loved best was playing outdoors. There were three children in the neighborhood, Johann, Peter, and Marion, who had come from Hamburg, and because Hamburg is a port city, they knew a lot more about ships than we did. They often played "ship" with us. The ship was our gymnastics tower with ladder, ropes, and iron bars. The children climbed around like sailors, and your mommy, who was still very small then, was the stewardess and was responsible for feeding the crew. The parents of our friends had been to Africa, and their gray parrot was from Africa too; it had a red tail, was called Gascon, and spoke. Marion declared every spring that the whole family would take a trip to Lisbon that year, but they never went. The boys taught us a game from Hamburg called "Akree"—that was a kind of hide-and-seek with touching. We played it in the long cellar corridor and the many dark cellar stalls under the house. An even nicer playground than the house and garden was the "little woods." That was a totally neglected lot, an overgrown thicket of trees, weeds, and bushes. The people who owned it never set foot in it, and when we entered it for the first time, we had to cut down and break all kinds of wild-growing stalks, or we wouldn't have been able to make our way. The area was also littered with old, unusable household items, broken plates, punctured pots, and a torn mattress from which the filling was oozing out. In the middle of the little wood, hidden from the street, was a small wooden structure. It was probably once, in reality, a stable, but to us children, it seemed very strange and wondrous, and we called it the "witches' house." The best thing about the witches' house was that it belonged to us children all alone. The grown-ups didn't go there because they didn't want to tear their clothes on the thorny underbrush.

Do you know the game "evil beast"? We played it in our garden in winter when it would get dark early, and the moon would shine on the white snow. One of the children was the "evil beast" and had to hide somewhere in the dark. The others walked about singing:

> We want to go for a nice long walk
> If only the "evil beast" does not come.
> The clock strikes one, the clock strikes two,
> The clock strikes three, the clock strikes four,
> The evil beast has not yet come.
> The clock strikes five, it's still not here,
> The clock strikes six, it's still not here. . . .

And the clock would keep on striking, and it still wouldn't come; until, all of a sudden, usually long after the stroke of midnight, it burst forth from behind an ambush with terrible howling and tried to grab one of the children. This winter evening game was "ghoulish," but that was exactly what we loved about it.

Sometimes we also played theater; but maybe I'll tell you about that some other time. I started this letter on the twenty-fifth, and to-day is already the twenty-ninth. I wrote a little bit every morning, but now I finally have to finish it. Only yesterday I didn't write between five and six in the morning as usual because I had to prepare Opa's birthday table. Fancy presents I didn't have to give, only practical things, and the main piece was a thick red and yellow soap cloth. But Opa appreciated it all anyway. We also had several visitors, and most of them brought flowers: carnations, gladiola, cyclamen, asters. The letter from the two of you arrived exactly on time, and today I received a letter from your Mutti. I thank her very much for it. I'm sure Helene would love to hear from you both. Go right ahead and send the letter to her home address, and her niece will bring it to her when she visits her in the hospital. That would be a nice diversion for her. Since she is no longer in extreme pain, she is very bored now. Uncle Siege recently sent a brief message via Red Cross. They are all well. But from Margarete, we haven't heard anything for a long time. Opa still wants to add a few words, therefore, now for you, dear monster, and your Mutti, best regards from the heart,

AUNT TRUDE

75

September 14, 1942

My dear little sister,

Thank you very much for the picture postcard of September 5, which arrived on the day before yesterday. Today is our High Holiday, and I shouldn't be writing, but I hardly have any time on other days. . . . And how much I would like to do nothing just for once, and yet, even today, I have sewing, darning to do; the beds have to be changed, among other things.—What you wrote about Vati and the company he has been keeping, he answered himself, without knowing it, several days after your letter arrived. With a deep sigh that everything was different and better in Finkenkrug since one didn't have to see any-body if one didn't want to, one didn't have to engage in all that talk but could just leave through the rear gate with the dog for a walk in the woods . . . He probably had, at that moment, the feeling that in the company of all these various acquaintances, he was no longer his own self as he once was. . . . This morning, I went to see Käthe, who was apparently very grateful for my visit. Since her divorce from her husband, she is very lonely. After such a long life together . . . The parting was probably more difficult for her than for him. Her only consolation is that it was the best for him, and she hopes that he is all right. From Georg arrived five letters within two weeks, dating back to various months. Send him my regards when you write and greetings from the heart for both of you,

TRUDE

76

September 27, 1942

My dear Hilde,

Many thanks for the "document of feminine vanity." Anything you write, I love to read. You haven't said anything for a long time about Sabine's eyesight. Does she still wear glasses? I'm happy that you look so young; as for myself, I believe that, outwardly at least, I have aged greatly these days. Outwardly only, but the exterior is perhaps all that counts about a woman. . . . right now I'm in the midst of an "insecure life" since Mrs. F. apparently had a falling-out with her children and is vacating her room here in order to keep the household for her widowed brother-in-law. She is joining him on October 1. This brother-in-law, a Mr. Kolmar, visited us recently. He sends regards to you. He said he was the father of Gertrud Kolmar, who also was a former friend of yours. Since Mrs. F. did the cooking for all of us, I don't know how it will all work out. The question is whether to keep the apartment, to move out, or to lease it. I plan to go to the community in the next days to clarify the situation.—Excuse this patched-up letter, but it was meant only as a sign of life until I find time to write a real, long letter again—but when? After Mrs. F's departure, more household duties than before will fall on me. Many, many greetings from the heart for both of you,

TRUDE

77

October 17, 1942

My dear sister,

As I'm writing "sister" I feel the full essence of the word—now that you are far away, as never before when we still saw each other and spoke in person—the word is for me all at once a treasure and a shelter. Like all your letters, also the last one with the picture (Sabine is a really big gosling; she seems to look more and more like you). I should have thanked you for it sooner, especially since I know that you are waiting for word from me—forgive me, I couldn't. It was not only the fault of the many business matters that now require my attention on top of everything else but most of all, the lack of calm, of peace. . . . I had every good intention of writing in the evenings at the post office, but then I was always too tired (how much I would have liked to sit down to a really long letter!). My tenants fill the apartment with nervousness, moaning, lamenting (and everywhere they leave the doors open); it is not that I don't feel sorry for them, but I would feel more strongly for them if they weren't so self-righteous, if they didn't regard their behavior as the only possible way. Oh, it's all so depressing! (I appear to them, I notice it, as someone outside the community of "normal human beings.") My solace is Hilde Benjamin, who visits frequently, my work companion, and your and Suse's letters. Be more "generous" than I; write again soon! With a loving heart for both of you!

TRUDE

78

October 31, 1942

My dear Monster!

Today I already have a really bad conscience at a quarter after five in the morning: I can't write you a long, beautiful letter as I do every year. It is not lack of wanting or of love but time. Tomorrow new tenants will be moving in here, three ladies. They'll be staying in the two front rooms, a large and a smaller one. And I'm back in the room I had before, which has now been vacated by Mrs. Fuchs. But I had to clean out the two front rooms, empty all closets, and most of all, I had to find room for all the books from two libraries—that was quite a bit of work.

So you must content yourself this time with a greeting card. I wish you—most of all, joy . . . much sunshine in your young life so you can give something of this warmth and brightness to your mother. To her, many thanks for the cards of October 19 and 25. For both of you, best regards and constant thoughts,

AUNT TRUDE

79

November 7, 1942

Dear little sister,

I hope the "monster" isn't angry with me that even on her birthday she had to content herself with a mere postcard, and her Mutti gets a letter. But today I have some mental and physical peace and am, therefore, able to write. A week ago, unfortunately, I didn't have this. (The doorbell just rang, and I had to exchange a few words with the landlady.)

And before I got started, one of the new tenants called me to show me that her radiator was leaking, and we first had to look for a shallow dish to place under it. On this occasion I entered the room for the first time since I had leased it to her—and I was horrified. This tenant is a well-meaning woman, but she is a little simpleminded and infantile. She's a Christian, and although she's in her thirties, she's a member of some religious girls' group. Despite the fact that she's home every morning until one o'clock, an indescribable disorder reigns in her room ("the comb is literally in the butter"); I wouldn't and couldn't hold it against her, for I too am not "free of guilt and fault"; but . . . the wall decorations! The wallpaper, the mirror, the picture frames, all have been papered over with postcards of verses and quotations from the Bible, in black and red writing; then there is a pyrography on wood, a white cardboard cross with the word "Jesus" imprinted in silver letters, a glass with artificial roses on the chest of drawers . . .

ghastly! I have always been able to look at the representation of a beautiful Madonna without discomfort, but to see this tasteless, huge cardboard cross on my wall and not be able to say anything, that took a lot of swallowing. I'm sure that many genuine, mentally more competent Christians would reject such pulp manifestations of their faith as much as I do, especially in such an amassment, such a hodgepodge. . . .

Now something different. I just had to write this still fresh impression, this horror, off my soul. . . .

What makes you think that your letter of October 28 was somewhat boring? It couldn't be for the reason alone that it contained this French quotation with which I was not familiar and which is as charming as it is true. I'm really happy for you and completely without envy; according to this, I too am only in my early twenties. . . . (Again, interruption: a tenant comes in to ask me for help in getting food ration stamps and to borrow a flat iron.)

After all, I, too, had "vingt ans" not so long ago. . . . But this is all over now; the zenith has been crossed, and this companionship, which we had both already called friendship, may be my sunset. For weeks now, I have been taking my breakfast communally. At lunchtime, to be undisturbed, I have been withdrawing into a stall-like corner in the work hall. Since he discovered me there one day and kept me company, he now comes almost daily, and since there's only one chair, he sits on a low tool box, which is as soot covered as his overalls. We talk for half an hour until it toots. And last Sunday afternoon, he was here. We sat together on the green living-room sofa, in front of us polished glasses and soft yellow chrysanthemums in the Chinese vase, and we polished off the last bottle from Finkenkrug. . . . and there were no disappointments, nothing that was strange between us, as sometimes is the case during such visits. . . .

But the most beautiful part was still to come. . . . did I ever write to you about an anatomy textbook (it belonged to Ella's husband) that contained an illustration of a male androgyne with secondary female characteristics? Well, we have such an "androgynous companionship with secondary erotic characteristics"; the latter came to the fore only during the two days that followed. While he didn't exactly stay out of my way on Monday and Tuesday, he did avoid talking to me and did not seek me out, either at my machine or in my stall. He also avoided any mention of our time together (and in response I did the same); in short, it was as if we had spent the night together, rather than the afternoon, and did not want to face up to it the following day. By Wednesday the dust had settled on the whole affair so to speak. At any rate, he appeared [The last page is missing.]

You see, I also have pleasures. . . . only they are not unclouded, which is neither his nor my fault. . . . Meanwhile, I had another free day, on November 6. I invited Hilde B. for the evening. We spoke about the dear child, and I read to her the relevant passages from your letter. If only I could see the "little monster" just once again and talk to her!

Today came your card from Sch. You can imagine how happy it made me. It was written on that same November 2 when I too was not alone.

Be happy—in spite of everything. . . . [Ending is missing.]

80

November 18, 1942

Hilde, dear sister!

Your letter of the fifth of this month gave me a great longing for the little monster! I felt doubly sorry that I hadn't been able to write her a really beautiful birthday letter. But why shouldn't I still do that now? Nowadays, deliveries of all kinds of goods are delayed due to the war; so why shouldn't I still deliver my letter even if with some delay? Maybe it'll work out this Sunday; last Sunday I was so "cracked up" that, in the afternoon, after cleaning my room and washing my stockings, I did something I haven't allowed myself in a long time: that is, absolutely nothing. I did what I often used to do in Finkenkrug. I sat on the sofa and turned off the light. And then I meditated in the dark. . . . And I placed—what I rarely have time for in the light—I placed the measure of eternity against all things and all that is happening. . . . and much of what we deem important, what occupies us so exclusively, what animates us, our own esteemed person included,

all that collapsed. . . . "Nations perish, so God may live!" These words
by Saint-Just came to my mind. Later I fell asleep in the dark because
I was too tired, but this quiet meditation did me a lot of good; it was
as if it gave me strength. Your letters too do that to me again and
again. I thank you from the heart. For both of you a thousand greetings!

TRUDE

81

November 22, 1942

My dear Monster,

I just finished cleaning my room—I have time for that only once a
week, and that's on Sundays. In the afternoon, I have to do ironing, and
now I want to see if I can finish a letter to you before lunch. Your
mommy's letter of November 5 made me really "homesick" for Püppi,
and it made me think that I should write the letter I hadn't been able
to write for her birthday and that I should absolutely still send it: so
here it is.

Your mommy wrote to me about your birthday, but she didn't tell
me at all whether you invited any friends from school. Children's par-
ties were always a major event for us. The first school friend who invited me was called Tula Quittmann. Her birthday was on January 27,
the same day as the Kaiser's. That was a very pleasant arrangement. We
were dressed in our good clothes already in the morning, went only for
an hour to class for the Kaiser's birthday celebration, and we didn't
have any homework; for the afternoon, we went to Tula's house and
celebrated her birthday. For lunch, we had vegetable soup or, as we
called it, "soup with everything in it." This was followed by an
omelette. And since I was still little, I thought that all families had
such a meal that day, even the Kaiser himself, that this was the Kaiser's
birthday meal. There's something else that I believed. (Aunt Trude
was a very dumb six-year-old, you'll say.) Some of the parents would
come to the school party for the Kaiser and among them was the

colonel of our Westend regiment, Herr von Kuczkowski! His three daughters (funny that I should remember their names to this day: Stefanie, Dagmar, and Dolly) went to our school. So the colonel, in parade uniform, in blue and red and gold, was given a place of honor among the fathers and mothers. When we left the auditorium at the end of the ceremony and walked past the parents, I made a deep curtsy in front of him for I believed that this high-ranking officer was the Kaiser (he would have had a lot to do and tear himself into lots of little pieces had he wanted to be at every school party in honor of his birthday!). Well, I thought that because I couldn't understand how one can celebrate a birthday without the birthday child present in person. I don't remember much about Madam Director's speech or the poems the older girls recited, but I remember very well the afternoons at Tula Quittmann's, even the tangerine salad we had in the evening. (In the afternoon, the children had hot chocolate, and usually a "colorful" bowl was passed around with chocolate marshmallows, éclairs, biscuit cakes, and other wonderful things—have your Mutti describe to you these delicacies, if you don't know them.) The deepest impression of that day, however, was left by the following: I went home alone at eight o'clock at night, and when I came to Branitz Square, I saw a pillar of light rising above an empty lot into the dark night sky. Today I know it was a rocket, which was set off on the empty lot in honor of the day. But at the time, I had never seen anything like it, and I took the pillar of light to be a divine apparition. Did you ever see fireworks? I always enjoyed them very much, especially the Roman candles and the rockets shooting up red, blue, and green phosphorescent balls.

Tell your Mutti I received a letter from the Junge not too long ago, written on our Mutti's birthday. Judging from his writing, he is quite content; he writes mainly about "gardening and agriculture." I assume that your Mutti has written to him recently, and I too will answer him soon.

Dear Pipkin, this letter is neither as long nor as beautiful as my earlier birthday letters, but you will settle for this one, won't you? With very best regards from the heart for you and your Mutti,

YOUR AUNT TRUDE

By the way, Helene is back home again.

82

December 4, 1942

Dearest sister!

For that's what you are, the sister dearest to me. Many thanks for your "happy Sunday" letter and the card of the twenty-sixth of this month, which followed yesterday. The mood in which your letter was written made me outright glad; it was almost as if I experienced myself what made you so happy. Memories rose up. . . . Should I regret that all that's left for me are memories? On the contrary, I'm happy to have them; though they may not be imbued with the ardor of summer, they still are warming like a fire in the hearth, which feels good on cold days. A man once said to me—well, he expressed it differently, simpler, but to explain his words I would have to recount the whole conversation—at any rate, in essence, he said, under the present circumstances, he thought of preparing for his old age because he was no longer capable of the experience of creating beautiful memories for his future. I believe, though, that few younger people regard their lives at any given moment in such a light. But maybe it's not so wrong to do that every once in a while. . . . "Yes, Luise, this is a wide field," said Effi Briest's father. Excuse this philosophical commentary, and on a postcard at that. Many, many greetings from the heart for both of you!

TRUDE

83

December 5, 1942

[Letter to Georg Chodziesner; beginning is missing.] Now you haven't had any news from here for a long time, but I hope that Hilde has been in contact with you. Your monthly letters are suddenly "drifting in" pretty much one after the other; in September, for example, came three with the same mail. The last one that arrived recently was the one from Mutti's birthday. I'm sure (and it seems that letters too give that impression) that horticulture, even if it isn't your actual profession, gives you a certain satisfaction, since it is like working for something that is growing, alive, not something soulless, sterile, but something that literally "bears fruit." In the summertime, when I was working for several weeks "with the men," I had the opportunity to wander off during break into a small, overgrown lot; there I stretched out in the grass between mullein and nettles, and the little bit of green and sun made me happy. . . . By the way, I'm working with the men at my own request; I almost would say out of my own absolute power. I desperately wanted to get away from the clatter, chatter, and patter that seem to be an inevitable side effect of a women's division and longed for a more "quiet existence," and since they were a man short in the men's division, I filled in without being asked, and the supervisor approved retroactively the fait accompli. For a few weeks, all was refreshingly quiet around me until it turned out that the work was, in the long run, too hard for me after all, and I unfortunately had to go back to the women. By the way, I'm on good terms with all the other women workers, but I don't cultivate a closer relationship with them; the men, on the other hand, welcomed me into their circle. I'm "one of them," and with one of them, the work relationship developed into a companionship and the companionship into a friendship. (It just occurs to me that you might think what is not the case—this companion is all of twenty-two years old, though unusually mature for his age.)

And I will be turning forty-eight in a few days! "Time passes; the light burns down." And I don't really feel that old. [Ending is missing.]

84

December 12, 1942

Hilde, dear sister,

Your letter of the tenth arrived today; I was getting a bit worried and was relieved when I recognized your typescript. Nothing was happening here on the tenth, absolutely nothing. I sat alone in my room and thought of those who used to celebrate with me. . . . but to make an announcement beforehand to my tenants or coworkers is not like me—I prefer quiet. . . . (I wouldn't have known anything about the birthday of my tenant Mrs. B. either had she not given a hint with the doorpost: "I didn't really want anybody to know, but my colleagues found out anyway that my birthday is on the twenty-fifth.") I saw Lenchen recently. She is still limping laboriously even with a cane and is still in pain. Who knows whether it will get much better. . . . I feel sorry for her. . . . Do you really think your daughter has less imaginative talent than you? Her spelling speaks against such an assumption. "Geburztag"—I think this is wonderful, perhaps the most beautiful word in your entire letter: how new and fresh it looks, and how old and worn appears "Geburtstag" [birthday] by contrast! My best thanks to the monster for these lines. Did I thank you for the card of November 26? I believe so, for I wrote to you after the late delivery for Bienelein's "Geburztag." A week ago, I wrote to the Junge by airmail. I hope you have written to him in the meantime.

Tuesday, a new tenant is moving in, and I have to get the room ready. But I'll write in greater detail soon. Many, many loving greetings from

TRUDE

Dec. 13/Your card of November 11 just arrived.

85

December 15, 1942

Hilde, dearest sister,

Now I want to attempt writing to you. Attempt . . . because I don't know if it will work. I was sick in bed for two days, not actually sick, but completely exhausted, faint and weary. I was reading a little in bed; then I slept and slept day and night; now I'm feeling like somebody who has recovered from a long illness. I had hoped to be able to go back to work tomorrow morning, even if it isn't going quite as usual.

I say "hope." This is a manner of speaking which slipped inadvertently from my pen. As incredible as it may sound: the way to work in the graying dawn, the daily routine, the drudgery (for that's what it is) over something I shall never completely master, the total fatigue every night, all this I should regard as coercion, as slavery, as something repugnant, and I should in my inner being beat against it as against a wall until my brow runs with blood; instead, whenever I have traversed the two courtyards and have squeezed myself through the narrow opening in the lattice door and have entered the hall with the big machine and the dim, blurry light, the piles of waste cardboard and a car blocking the way, I feel: "At home again." "At home." That's the way it is. More at home there than in Speyererstrasse 10. For here, my tenants make themselves at home, strangers who have taken possession of everything that is mine, my things, our things, and nothing belongs to me anymore. Perhaps my room still does. But only when all are out of the house. For as soon as they are home, they usually gather in the kitchen, and I can't begrudge them the lively exchange, perhaps not even that topic of conversation which remains almost always the same: their fate. . . . But it all penetrates the locked door and forces out my quiet and calm and dignity and the silent strength I have gathered about me and to which I must hold on. . . . And on occasion, a chore needs to be done that is outright enjoyable, yes indeed enjoyable! . . .

My friend, Dr. H., who was a Spinoza scholar, spoke to me one day about the concept of freedom of the human will in the midst of unfreedom. I said that I understood this very well from my own experience. For it was not up to me to accept or reject this factory work that has been imposed on me; I had to acquiesce and carry it out. But I was free in my inner soul to adopt a negative or a positive attitude toward it, to approach it willingly or unwillingly. At the moment when I *affirmed* it in my heart, the pressure was lifted from me. I was determined to regard it as a learning experience and to learn from it as much as I could. In this way I was free in the midst of my unfreedom.

This is how I want to walk under my fate, may it be as tall as a tower, may it be as black and oppressive as a cloud. Even though I don't know it yet: I have affirmed it in advance; I have surrendered to it in advance, and therefore, I know that it will not crush me; it will not find me meek and small. How many of those who are now collapsing in the face of an overwhelming fate have asked themselves whether they might not deserve this punishment, that they might owe some form of atonement? I was not worse in what I did and desired than other women. But I knew that I did not live my life the way I should have and was always ready to atone. And all the suffering I had to bear and still will have to bear, I shall accept as punishment, and it will be just. I shall bear it without moaning, and I shall find somehow that it belongs to me and that I was born to endure and somehow overcome it and that I shall have grown in my innermost being because of it.

This strength in the face of fate, this growing toward that which is yours: that it may never be more powerful than your own heart, that, my dear sister, is what I wish you for your birthday,

TRUDE

P.S. I wrote you on the thirteenth that your postcard of November 11 finally arrived; there's nothing mysterious about it; it is so crumbled and torn, it probably got stuck somewhere, maybe in the mailbox.

86

December 21, 1942

Dear Hilde,

My letter had hardly gone out when, as usual, your two cards of the seventh and tenth arrived. My thanks to you and the unknown cosigner. This time I'm not writing by any means: "Nothing new from here," for there is something new. I have changed my workplace and in the process slithered from Lichtenberg to Charlottenburg on Wilmerdorferstrasse. It's a forty-minute walk, which is now, since the weather is dry, rather pleasant. It's also pleasant because I start an hour later and leave the house at 7:15 instead of ten to six. As a result, I'm now always wonderfully rested.

My previous work required a special practical ability, my present work—though I stay in the same "line" of work—requires special neatness and precision, and the latter is much more to my liking than the first. My new female coworkers laughed when I said I feel like a blacksmith who has been promoted to watchmaker. . . . Among those coworkers is, by the way, the sister of Dr. Bamberger. Are you by any chance in contact with him? You know I was not exactly his friend. . . . During the holidays, I hope to have time to write more extensively. Meanwhile, greetings from the heart to you and the monster,

YOUR SISTER TRUDE

87

December 26, 1942

My dear sister,

Actually, I should have waited until tomorrow, as I had wanted to, with writing to you. But what can I do if I'm sitting here this morning, in a still disorderly room, and am thinking of you so vividly, and I feel like writing you? So I'm taking out a sheet of fine writing paper, a gift from Martha (Martha is to Suse what Helene is to us), and I begin. (I just remember that I still have to wash the vestibule floor before mealtime, but that can wait.)

I already wrote to you about my "change of scenery," namely, that I slithered from Lichtenberg to Charlottenburg with regard to my workplace and that this exchange was more of gain for me than a loss. I already wrote a card to you about this on Monday. There's only one disadvantage about my new area of activity: I was unable to have my old crew transferred with me. Not that my present colleagues, men and women (there are more of the latter than the first) are in any way "unpleasant" toward me. By no means, they are even much nicer than "my men" were in the beginning. But the atmosphere . . . the tone . . . These ladies, among whom is, by the way, besides Dr. Bamberger's sister, also a cousin of the wife of Justice Wronker, they have obviously been psychologically pampered by the milder, western climate [the western part of Berlin, trans.], whereas the raw storms of the eastern part of Berlin fortified the hearts of "our men." All joking aside, or rather there is some truth in this . . . These moaning and groaning women probably led comfortable bourgeois lives, surrounded by "every amenity." The fact that they can no longer live in this style is certainly cause for lament. (Of course, only one of many . . .) The men in Lichtenberg, by contrast, didn't come from such privileged, upper-class homes, though many did well in the old days; among them were several merchants, a butcher, a waiter, a shoemaker, a local civil servant, a mortician. The only one with a higher education was my companion, but he was perhaps positioned more than the others in an "insecure life." Even though I had little liking for their frequently off-color innuendo, the former waiter's suggestive, or not so suggestive, remarks (he was, by the way, our most competent transport worker), I sometimes wish he were here to pour a little paprika on all that chatter. . . . I feel in this, as I said, rather nice company of ladies out of place. My hand itches sometimes to give those who are totally down a friendly, encouraging box in the ribs. For the time being, I keep to myself though since I'm still new. Once I have established right of residence, I'll be likely not as tolerant. For I realize that I must close my inner being off from these "climatic influences" if I want to preserve my mental fortitude. When I think of my companion and his soot-covered coat in this environment! He would probably not say a word. . . .

I'm sure you already know that it's he whom I miss most. "I once *had* a companion!" For I don't know whether I still have him or not. That saying good-bye was difficult for me is not surprising, but that *his* voice should have had a slight, almost imperceptible tremor during the last exchange of a few words in his workshop did surprise me, and I'd almost say I was touched. After all, I may have been more to him than I believed, than I commanded myself to believe. A forty-eight-year-old woman and a twenty-two-year-old man form a strange yoke team; amazing is that it trotted so well together. There was nothing motherly or sisterly or brotherly or any other "ly" that usually guides such affairs. By the way, he wouldn't hear of a final good-bye. My new workplace is near the place where he lives, and I have already been to see him once. He promised, if possible, to come over on one of the holidays—will he do it? Aren't we already distancing ourselves gradually? Even in the factory, we didn't speak with each other all that often or all that much. It was enough to know that the other was there and that one could pour one's heart out when needed. Well . . . I want to be content and grateful that at my age I was still presented with such a gift, a much greater rarity than a love between eighteen and twenty-four. "Be it as it may, it was beautiful still!" And perhaps . . . Suse sent me a volume of Bergengruen's short stories for my birthday. (I very much appreciate his sparse, chronicle-like narrative style.) The last story in the book mentions the image of a jasper-adorned ring and a broken anchor cut into a stone with the inscription "Et tamen spero" "And still I hope."—Et tamen spero.

Now to something else. To you and Sabine. Do you have a tree? I'm sure you do. I spoke with Hilde [Benjamin] the other day about the edible ornaments we used to like best. She thought it was chocolate rings with white and colored poppy seeds. I thought it was Russian confectioneries and little quince sausages. An ornament that was not edible and probably existed only in our house—do you remember?— were two cotton crocodiles which Grandma Sch. gave us as a gift, and they crawled over the branches of the fir tree every Christmas, a zoological oddity. What does the "monster" like best? She must have inherited her liking for harmonicas from her Aunt Trude; I always had a harmonica and played it quite well, and I remember taking it on a wagon ride in Arvedshöf and then would blow it by popular demand.

December 27

I had nursed a secret hope that someone would come and celebrate the day with me—who, I don't know (maybe my companion . . .). But nobody came, and now it is not likely that anybody will still come. So I want to tell you that I'm thinking of you here in my loneliness, of you and the child—and I'm imagining how you might be spending the afternoon. I wish I were there with you—no, I'm with you, if not in body, then in spirit, with my heart. I hold your hand in mine,

TRUDE

88

January 5, 1943

Hilde, dear sister!

Thank you for the letter of the nineteenth and the Christmas card— both arrived yesterday—many thanks also to all the undersigned, especially the pencil writer. I spent the holidays in, "lonely, not alone" inside my four walls, except for a visit from Hilde B. on the twenty-sixth and a visit I paid myself to Käthe. She's always happy to see someone with whom she can speak about her divorced husband. Her thoughts are constantly with him, but he doesn't write (probably not to make the separation more difficult). And so I was wondering whether you, since you were also a friend of his, are still in contact with him? She's hoping to hear something about him this way. But I was, of course, unable to answer her questions. . . . Strangely perhaps, I myself feel most lonely in the company of my new work crew. I'm withdrawing more and more since I noticed that my views are generally not taken seri-

ously and that they are regarded as the eccentric statements of an adolescent who doesn't believe himself what he's saying and says it only to
shock and offend the adults. This is how unimaginable it is for these
people to take a positive, affirmative attitude toward that which is
happening. And should we not somehow welcome even our separation? Would the two of us ever have become as close as we are now if
fate hadn't placed us so far apart? That the one may remain and the
other may change, that is what I wish for the new calendar year,

YOUR TRUDE

89

January 10, 1943

[To Georg Chodziesner; beginning is missing.] Will this card reach
you by March 4? I hope so. It is meant to bring you my best birthday
wishes for everything you wish for yourself—from the depth of my
heart. (Does a card have a heart? It has mine. . . .) I haven't heard from
you for a while; the last was dated from Mutti's birthday; your descriptions of "gardening and agriculture" always make me a bit homesick. . . . For Finkenkrug . . . Since mid-December, I have a new workplace in Charlottenburg; in the evening I ride home, but in the
morning I walk through the quiet, snow-covered streets under the
pale moon. . . . My female colleagues don't get my pleasure in this "er-
satz nature"; they don't understand why I don't always take a ride.
They are almost all older women, and I really miss "my men"; the work
here is, of course, less strenuous. And cleaner. I always feel like a blacksmith who has been promoted to watchmaker. [Ending is missing.]

90

January 13, 1943

Dear little sister!

Thanks for the cards of December 27 and January 1; they arrived together day before yesterday. What you write made me very happy; I'm

only sorry that my birthday letter arrived so late. The sister of our family doctor also had a letter from her brother on the day before yesterday; she had told him about our work together, and he now asked for the addresses of my brother and sisters and Uncle Siege. I didn't give her yours but said that I left it up to you to give him the desired addresses, some of which I don't have—between the two of us: I presume if you wanted to get in contact with him, you would have done so already. The sister is, by the way, one of the most pleasant people; otherwise, however, the gulf between me and the work crew is imperceptibly widening more and more, which is unpleasant, but it can't be helped. ("The woman is the nicest fellow in the whole firm," the worker U. in Lichtenberg, a former waiter, once said about me behind my back. Here the judgment about me is, I'm sure, drastically different.) And this, even though I belong "by background" to the same social circles as my present female coworkers, whereas the men in L. came from socially less-privileged classes. With the latter, I was able to connect, while I find it impossible with these. Could it be perhaps that race is a stronger factor than class, and that those men were Jews in good as well as bad times, whereas *these* here, who seem assimilated in an annoying, purely superficial way and, in part, cannot come to terms with the fact that they are Jews, since they hadn't been for decades? Possible . . . At any rate, I'm quite lonely, and even though "the strong are mightiest alone," any break in the solitude coming from you and Bienelein still makes me happy.

YOUR TRUDE

91

January 24, 1943

Hilde, dear sister!

Today, Sunday afternoon, as a reward, so to speak, for having been good about my mending chores, I opened up once again *The Battle with the Demon;* when I put it down, I saw the price 7.50 on it, written a bit awkwardly by you, and I was almost a little touched. . . . I'm now getting to read a little more (though not much; housework takes priority), not only because I have more time but especially because I'm less tired and mentally more receptive. I also have been told that I look better; I believe so myself. . . . All this is strange since I was much happier in my previous position—*here*, I'm meeting once again people from those circles among whom I felt so little at home, was even unhappy, when I was twenty years old; today I understand completely why. . . . Certainly, many of these ladies could be regarded as mostly very charming and likable, but they seem older than I by a generation, even if they are not. Their conversations often bring to my mind what was said about the returned royalists after the fall of Napoleon: they learned nothing and forgot nothing. Well, I too have forgotten nothing, but I believe I have learned a great many things. Especially one thing: *Amor fati*—love of fate. The seed of this was, I believe, always in me, maybe already as a green shoot; but only now is it flowering and bursting forth. . . . Thank you for your card of the tenth of this month; it arrived yesterday. Anything that comes from you makes me happy; but—may I be so immodest and hope for another, longer letter?

For you, my dear ones, everything bright and cheerful!

TRUDE

92

January 26, 1943

My dear little sister,

In my last card, I was so "immodest" to request a letter from you, something longer in writing, and lo and behold, my request was granted that very evening. I was looking for something in my bookcase and came across your "Greek Travels," and I read it before going to sleep. I must say it again: it is wonderful. In this small work, you rose above yourself, so to say, and became a poet. Of course, the experience was exhilarating; what you saw was overwhelming. But your motto is right: the essential thing about a journey is the personality of the person undertaking it. (Vati and I often discussed this. For example, Max Prenzlau with his buffalo cart in the South African savanna experienced absolutely nothing, whereas Uncle Alex experienced all sorts of strange things doing no more than standing guard in Kulm as a soldier.) My last—and most beautiful—journey was to Hamburg, Lübeck (on the trail of the Buddenbrooks), and Travemünde. The most indelible impression was left by a wintry night on a solitary beach. The diary of my journey consists of seven poems, some of which, I think, are among my very best.

In connection with such things—journeys, memories—I have been thinking about why it is that most people are unable to store up a large stock of joy, of happiness, from which they can nourish themselves in days of want, of drought. I assume that many women are granted the gift of a great love experience; why does the luster radiating from such occasions only rarely illumine their daily, routine lives? Can a treasure collected at twenty not last into the forties? Or maybe it often is not as great and rich as I imagine it? And why should the splendors of a love affair, the greatest happiness, the enduring bond between two lovers vanish more quickly from the heart's memory than the memory of an encounter between two people that was often only of short duration? Only because the constant, the abiding exercises a numbing effect, and what it touches turns gray as the dust on an object that nobody cleans from time to time? Be that as it may . . .

And thus I'm not (somewhat to my own surprise!), not really unhappy that the novel "My Companion and I" did not continue after a somewhat abrupt ending. This friendship had something of the glimmer, the vacillating flicker of a love affair; it's better if the flame is extinguished in one fell swoop than that it should tire gradually, die down, smolder, and burn out. . . . During our last talk at the factory, I wanted to say good-bye forever, but he wouldn't hear of it. He spoke of the abiding bond between us and of meeting again. What was, was beautiful and will never lose its splendor and strength in the course of everyday life.

A few weeks before my departure, I showed him a picture of myself when I was eighteen (the one Mutti had made at Wertheim's). He examined it closely; then he looked at me and said: "The essential has remained." If he were right, I would be pleased (and so would you). I almost believe that he was right. . . .

I just remember something else from our last conversation. (You see, I'm developing into a regular Büchmann; only I'm collecting the "winged words" of my companion.) We spoke about our history, about traditions, and he said: "I believe in the past only inasmuch as I carry it within me." I feel the same way. What doesn't live in the blood, in the soul, no amount of goodwill, of thinking with the brain, can make completely my own; I only have what I already am. Andersen's ugly little duckling didn't have to know anything about swans; it carried it within itself, and one day it was there. The reason why much of that which is traditional, many a laudable custom, cannot be revived, much to the dismay of those who wish to do so, is that none of our contemporaries carry even a trace of it within themselves. This is also true for the attempts to resuscitate religions that have long been dormant, whose rites and rhythms no longer beat in the hearts of thousands and are nothing more than letter and number in a history book. In my case, a piece of the past is so deeply grown into me that I couldn't tear it out without causing myself serious injury. . . .

Past. History. Sometimes I notice how many dates, names, facts, which at one time I could have cited in my sleep, have escaped from me meanwhile. I don't believe that my memory has gotten worse. Only this *living* of history is like a vast, overflowing river that has washed over everything I once *read*, flooded it and swept it away. Much lingers still somewhere; much is still adrift; much has sunk to the bottom. . . . I'm enclosing two pages from my "travel diary"—more Fantasy than Truth—and yet truth. I greet you and the dear child (whom I have totally neglected in this letter, but I hope she will forgive me),

TRUDE

1 enclosure (2 pages)

93

February 2, 1943

Who would have thought that I would get up again at 12:30 at night to write to my dear little sister. These hours between dreaming and waking were always reserved for a different kind of correspondence, one which I, however, at my age, am not likely to have again. . . . But I was already awake and feared that in the morning I might not be able to crawl out of the feathers early enough to write you a card, and I did want to let you know right away how much I enjoyed your letter of the nineteenth, found on returning home yesterday evening. And on the day before yesterday arrived your card of the twenty-fourth; this one was fast.

Nothing much new from here. Leo came to visit me last week. We spoke about something that ordinarily we would only skirt lightly: his marriage. He thinks that it wouldn't have broken apart so completely had he and his wife remained closer together spatially. I didn't tell him that I dared have secret doubts about that. . . . When he was twenty-five, he seemed to me a mature young man. Today I have the impression that, although a "nice" person and a "good" fellow, he has remained mentally and intellectually on the same level as he was then and has hardly gone through further development; when I look at his wife, by contrast, I see behind the youthful appearance an already strong and still increasing inner maturing. The question is whether this would have been stifled had they lived together constantly. . . . I don't believe so. . . . What do you think? . . . but maybe you don't know them well enough. . . . I hope to be able to write more soon. For the time being, thank you and greetings and a kiss for the "monster."

YOUR SISTER TRUDE

94

February 13, 1943

"My dearly beloved sister,"

This is how one used to write in days of old (and the way I still can write today): your card of the second of this month is here, making me happy as does everything you send me.

I'm also eagerly awaiting the letter you promised. I'll wait till it comes before I write in greater detail. But I must scold you now. I must unburden myself of something that weighs heavily on my heart. This is it: in your last letter, you told me about the holidays and that you were happy and still are "as far as possible." Now I hear that you wrote to Helene that you felt like sitting and crying the entire time. . . .

How does this go together? Certainly, I can imagine that both are possible, that one can be "walking on clouds one minute, down in the pit, at the same time" and yet . . . An ugly thought creeps in like a black, sticky snail: is it possible that you, maybe with the best intention of not wanting to make me sad, pretended to be cheerful and forward looking without really having it in you, and you were hiding your tears from me? I'm taken aback somewhat by this concealment, this not-letting-me-know. You remain without my help since I don't even know that help is needed. And I want so much to be of help; maybe I could. . . . Tell me the truth soon, the full truth, to your loving sister

TRUDE

95

February 20, 1943

My dear little sister,

The sun has just been setting, and I thought I'd read a few of Buber's *Tales of the Hasidim* for Oneg Shabbath. But after leafing through the book briefly, I decided to put off reading until later tonight and sat down at my writing table to answer your letter (of the seventh of this month) in quietude and with leisure. Do you know what made me especially happy? The "disturbances" you had to put up with while you were writing. Please return the "troublemaker's" greetings from my heart. I was somewhat disappointed since I missed on page two of your letter the details of the "experience" you mentioned on page one and about which Miss R. was so enthusiastic concerning the oral presentation. But I'm sure you will deliver it later. Even the few hints from you really made my mouth water.

"Man proposes, God disposes." In my last letter, I professed myself against sequels to finished novels, and I had declared mine to be absolutely concluded. Then on February 7 in the afternoon, probably just as you were writing to me, the bell rings, and the hero reappears on the scene. It was such a complete surprise to me that he wakes me from my afternoon nap, and I don't even have time to slip out of my old work clothes (still from cleaning chores) and into more appropriate attire. Equally unexpected was that he visited me again last Sunday. My whole theory about his being hurt and so on was wrong, as theories often are. Well, I'm pleased, but . . .

The but is this: after these tasty little bits, I feel doubly hungry for the good dish. As long as I thought that our separation was permanent, it was, strangely enough, not all that difficult to do without his daily presence. However, these short visits, which had to end before the conversation had a chance to move from externals to internals, stimulated the appetite without, so to say, without satisfying. For in the main, I let him tell me about the activities at my old factory. "Ever since I took a second husband, I love my first," a woman once said somewhere. Since I took my second job . . . I feel like someone in a strange land whose homeland is not particularly beautiful yet, nevertheless, was at home there and feels good about receiving news from there. I already told you that here in the West, the work and everything about it is much more pleasant than Lichtenberg; only one thing makes me unhappy: my coworkers. There are maybe one or two with whom I sometimes enter into conversation (Dr. B.'s sister is the nicest among them). But a relationship as it existed between me and my male coworkers at the "Big Machine" or with my companion of the late shift, an older man, does not exist here. The other men too regarded me as a colleague. They did me small favors when I asked for them, and I know they liked me. . . . While I was surrounded there by a sort of laconic friendliness, here I'm met occasionally with unconcealed aversion. Neither can I find here a vessel willing to receive what I have to give. (I'm not referring to my art "about which nobody knows nothing.") And so I was pleased to hear my companion report some news from "this little piece of home."

My life is, however, not completely without its joys. One is my morning walk. The sun is already on the rise when I set out. It's a wonderful feeling to turn around at the end of Pariserstrasse and look back at the Ludwig Church with its background of soft, distinct carmine and lilac colors. I used to see everything only in outline form, as silhouettes, like a paper cutting. It was only in Hamburg, along the landscape around the Alster River, that I learned to see with the eyes of a painter. When the evening would bring forth, as by magic, a mauve-colored sky above the water on the opposite riverbank, where the first lights from the Uhlahorst ferry house made it look like a fairy-tale castle. Swans would drift by slowly in search of a resting place. . . .

Do you know—perhaps from the Blue Book "The Quiet Garden"— the *Morning* by Runge? The picture is in the Hamburg art museum together with the wonderful works by Caspar David Friedrich. After having seen it many times, I pondered over it once on a gray day, and I was totally enchanted. In the murky light, it seemed to me to give off a unique, indescribable gleam. With nameless, sweet colors . . . I never forgot this impression to this day. . . . I had a position as governess which was not much to my liking, and still I enjoyed being in that city because it seemed so beautiful to me. It was this city I had in mind when I wrote the poem "The City" (collection *Welten*), and it almost seems to me that I can talk about it the way you talk about Greece. I remember an evening on the Stingfang; the *Cap Polonio* was anchored there with chimneys like red collars. . . . And the Fleete and the gilded steeple of the St. Catherine's Church and the green patina of Peter's Tower . . . And the city park and the botanical gardens and the huge lawn in the gardens around the mansions of Harvestehude, which were already covered with scylla and crocuses . . . And the seagulls at the Jungfernstieg . . . All this and much more is preserved in my memory as a gallery of beautiful pictures. . . . And all that which was repugnant and petty in that house, that, I hardly think about at all.

February 21

It is now 4:30 in the afternoon, and since nobody has come, I probably needn't expect anybody anymore. This morning arrived a rather dated letter from the Junge. Two more, no younger, I received recently; one was meant for my birthday. They all contained pretty much the same and said nothing. I sent him a birthday card by airmail at the beginning of January and hope it will arrive reasonably on time.

You say that you feel "now a strong desire to write." So do I. Sometimes I think that I might take it up in spite of the work, the lack of time, disquiet, fatigue. But of late everything that seems to want to take form just flutters away again. My last little work, a story, was created a year ago. I believe that if a new one should take form, it will in all likelihood again be a story. I'm actually just in the right mood, downcast and depressed about not being able to do anything as a poet. For (I might have mentioned this to you before) I never create from a feeling of euphoria or strength but always from a feeling of helplessness. Whenever I permit myself to follow a sudden inspiration, a creative impulse, I usually cannot sustain it: the fire dies down, the source dries out, and the poem remains a fragment. But when I begin a work from a state of helplessness, of despair, then I resemble someone at the start of a steep climb from the depth toward the summit; at first the goal is very distant, the view blocked, but as it progresses, the view grows wider and more beautiful. I don't weaken in the course of this gradual ascent as I do when I let myself be carried away by a sudden flash of imagination. What I begin is always completed, and the completed work does not sag toward the end as much poetry often does. (Mr. Cohn once said that my pieces always get better toward the end.) I must be able to tell myself: "I can't do anything anymore; my strength is exhausted; I won't accomplish anything"—then the hour has arrived. And since I had the patience to wait for it, there are no fragments floating around in my desk drawers.

Something funny just came to my mind that happened a few years ago. During an informal gathering following an evening of "Unheard Voices," where my verses were not recited, by the way, the writer Josefa Metz introduced herself to me. She sat down next to me and asked, among other things, whether I found creative work difficult or easy. "Difficult," I replied. She found it easy, she said. This and that Viennese newspaper had praised her work, and once she even won first prize in a Berlin Gasworks competition for an advertisement poem. "Just imagine, the first prize of the Berlin Gasworks," she repeated with enthusiasm and seemed unable to tear herself away from this wonderful memory. This story sprang to mind just so. . . .

Of two of my colleagues, one is an opera singer and the other a well-known actress who is also musically talented. At work the conversation once turned to this topic. "Nothing but celebrities and artistic talents," noted the cousin of the wife of Justice Wr., who sat next to me. "Only you and I, we are nothing and can do nothing." I listened without batting an eye. Some other time, though, she had said to me that I looked like I wrote poetry. I left the remark unanswered. . . .

That Sabine should be chubby and should like to eat, as you say, I can believe, and it makes me happy. That she should be impudent, I don't believe. She may be ill-behaved at times, but I can't imagine this turning into impudence. A monster can be bad, terrible, but not impudent. Being big and voracious, those are the true characteristics of a monster. Give her my regards from the heart, and for you with equal affection, from

Your sister,

TRUDE

LETTERS TO WALTER BENJAMIN
1934

❖

96

Finkenkrug, October 10, 1934
(Osthavelland), Manteuffelstr. 9–13
(Our street has been renamed and renumbered.)

Dear Walter,

I was very happy to be reading your handwriting again and, especially, to hear that you are feeling good where you are. Aunt Clara once told me—some time ago—that you were in Denmark but was unable to give any details. Otherwise, I would have sent you [my poetry collection] *Preußische Wappen (Prussian Town Coats of Arms),* all the more since I owe you the publication of "Wappen von Lassan" in the Swiss [paper] *Neue Rundschau,* meaning that your participation in the little work was assured. I am sending you under separate cover a booklet that has been published in a collection of similar little volumes of poems and which includes about twenty "Wappen" from my coats of arms book. I had been negotiating with the publisher back in early 1933 and also signed a contract; but due to the events, the actual publication of the little volume had been long delayed. You'll find the dates when the poems were written on one of the first pages; I wanted to make clear that I composed the "Wappen" at a time when regional poetry was not yet all the rage. Furthermore: (so you can see that I don't brush off good advice) You disliked the last stanza of "Wappen von Zinna," which you once published under the title "Apfel" ("Apple") in *Literarische Welt (Literary World),* and although I didn't cut it, I did change it; on the other hand, I did remove a link in "Wappen von Bocholt" which you thought was unnecessary. You probably hardly remember any of this. . . .

Of course, I would be happy if you of all people would write a critique, although you—who knows?—are likely to be a more severe critic than the one who has been assigned; but I am sure your understanding would be different, much deeper than that of a stranger. I would appreciate being informed about the publication of the review, since we get neither the *Frankfurter Zeitung* nor do I know anybody who does and could draw my attention to it.

Nothing new about us here; our hermit's life goes on as before. My father too appreciated your regards and returns them many times.

I just remember that I could send you, in addition, one of more recent poems: "Robespierre," of which I am particularly fond; whether you will like too, I can't tell, of course.

Now accept my thanks and greetings from the heart

GERTRUD

97

Finkenkrug, November 5, 1934

Dear Walter,

I'm not sure your last letter requires a reply; but its content stimulates a few remarks, nevertheless, which I don't want to let go stale until the time we'll meet again. I already wrote you—and will repeat it here— that and why I regret not having you as reviewer of my "coats of arms book"; your letter of October 18 was, at any rate, a little private presentation which I read attentively and gratefully. I don't want to talk much more about the "town coats of arms"—I am sure you're right about the "Wappen von Irlich"; I regard this poem myself as a changeling of mine (there's not much one can do about changelings), and I included it only at the request of an outsider. But I'd rather talk about something else, something that was new to me: I didn't know that the three collections of poems you mentioned were for you the alpha and the omega of new, creative poetry. I hold the works of these three poets myself in high esteem; but they remain somewhat alien to me: I admire them for a certain form. (And I probably have read too little of them to be able to accept them or reject them.) The one closest to me is probably Georg Heym; he and I chance to have written some verses about the same subject, that is, Robespierre's ride to the blood scaffold; his is called "Robespierre" (do you know it?), mine "Rue Saint-Honoré"—his house is still in existence or better, the house of his landlord Duplay, and is now number 398—nothing could be more different than these two poems. Among the German poets who might have influenced me are Rilke and Werfel, in both cases, various details from their works; in Rilke it's the "plastic" of the later poetry that attracts me. He has that from Rodin, from France, and I would say about myself—since no artist originates complete of himself like Athena from the head of Zeus—that I'm probably here and there descended form the French. After a long infertile period, I found my way back to poetry when I came back from Dijon in 1927, and my great moose in "Wappen von Allenburg" may not be an artificial imitation but (the zoologists may forgive me!) a natural offspring of Leconte de Lisle's mighty bird in "Le Sommeil du Condor (*Poèmes barbares*)." I know I owe a lot especially to Leconte de Lisle, but he probably just extracted from me what was in me anyway, rather than implanting something that was alien to me. Whatever I have been reading of modern French poetry must have stirred little in me since, at the moment, I cannot remember any of it. My "youngest" is Paul Valéry, some of whose poetry, especially the shorter pieces, are quite alien to me but whose other, longer poems I admire, love, and find by no means very difficult to understand. When I walk through a forest, I can no longer pass a young, somewhat twisted beech tree without thinking of the poem from "Au Platane": "et ce hêtre formé de quatre jeunes femmes" without seeing these four women who support the crown; oftentimes it's only three. "La Fileuse" in *Album des vers anciens* is among the things most beautiful to my mind. My attitude toward poetry is probably similar to yours: it happens frequently that I don't like the entire work of a poet but like to read select poems over and over again. That's how I feel about Rimbaud, who as a human being repels me more than he attracts me, whose "Dormeur du Val" I once found somewhere and haven't been able to find since. Several years ago, an old beggar used to come regularly to our house; he looked completely ravaged by alcohol, but I always gave him something because his face seemed to me like that of a twin brother of Verlaine.—And then there is Milton and his *Paradise*

Lost (when I read it, I always felt annoyed about Klopstock's unfortunate *Messiah,* which probably has spoiled biblical epics for many Germans); do you know this work? I think it is wonderful, especially the depiction of hell, the Pandemonium. This reminds me that you were once a great admirer of Spitteler; was that a passing phase? He is, of course, not a "pure" poet.

Please don't take this letter to be a profound discussion that aspires to any value, neither take it as a poet's creed but simply as what it is: a chat, stimulated by your last letter.—My father sends greetings; I wish you a friendly, enjoyable winter in Paris.

Yours,

TRUDE

LETTERS TO JACOB PICARD
1937–1939

✦

98

November 14, 1937
Finkenkrug (Osthavelland),
Manteuffelstrasse 9–13

My dear Dr. Picard,

When I picked up the *C. V. Zeitung* recently, with great interest, and was reading your essay about the creative moment "without thinking anything evil" and suddenly saw my name after that of Mombert and before Dostoyevsky—can you imagine how that makes me feel? It's hard to describe—but maybe that's how Andersen's "ugly, little duckling" felt when it ended up among the swans and recognized when it saw its image on the surface of the water that it was a swan as well. . . . I thank you with all my heart for the printed words as well as the written words in your letter. Now, far be it from me to pretend false modesty and to protest that I don't deserve the high praise which you have bestowed on my verses. . . . No, for you see, I really didn't go through that great, artistic struggle as other poets did—this I confess frankly— my struggle was always merely to be a strong, good-hearted woman, and to hear now from the mouth of an expert that my art inadvertently grew along with it makes me happy in my innermost being. I hope this confession won't lessen your esteem of my word. It made me happy when, some time ago, Mrs. Feld told me that your poems and mine would be recited on the same evening, and it made me even happier when she told me that the pleasure was mutual. . . . For I care little about being the foremost star illuminating the sky of minor stars, and I'm sure you don't either! Oh, how I would have liked to have written to you: "I'm honored by your words of praise, my dear doctor;

but Germany has many Jewish women poets more eminent than I am. . . ."—You know very well yourself, I couldn't write such a thing, that my words would only be a courtesy lie, and it would be very sorry to think that. . . .

My concerned letter of the eighth of this month, which crossed your letter, appeared in retrospect rather foolish; but as I wrote you, I have recently had cause for bemoaning the loss of various pieces of mail sent to me. . . . "Burned child shies away from the fire."

Now permit me once more to thank you from the heart for all your good words which you are willing to put in for me and my work before publication. Be assured that I am looking forward even now to repeat my thanks personally in December. With my best regards, I call myself by the name of honor you have bestowed on me,

Your colleague

GERTRUD CHODZIESNER

99

January 26, 1938
Tel.#: Falkensee 2170
Finkenkrug, 1/16/38
Manteuffelstr. 9–13

My very dear Doctor,

Since I don't have your address, I am sending this letter to Mrs. Feld with the request to forward it to you.

After I had put down the receiver last Sunday, I would have called you right back had I known your number. For it occurred to me that I might have hurt your feelings by refusing your visit and that I should have asked you to come in spite of the planned family gathering. But, first of all, it is not customary within the wider family circle to discuss my "poetic activity.". . . Besides the fact that the small children would have been bored by the conversation and would have demanded attention. For me to retire with the two of you to a quiet corner would have been impossible since my guests expect me to be housewife and maid at the same time.

I hope you can understand the situation I am in and won't begrudge me the rebuff.

I am writing only today since I am still thinking of coming to your reading despite the fact that I said earlier I couldn't come. But I am still unable to sit in a chair for hours without pain. I am very sorry about that.

In the hope, my dear Doctor, to hear from you again during the week before your departure, I send you my best regards,

Yours very truly,

GERTRUD CHODZIESNER

100

Finkenkrug, Osthavelland
Manteufelstrasse 9–13
July 7, 1938

My very dear Doctor!

My thank-you note for your kind farewell notice from Berlin follows only today, quite late; the months have gone by for me—I must say, unfortunately—rather quickly. I hope your days have been as well as is possible under the circumstances. Now I have a request: would you kindly return to me the verse cycles "Tierträume" and "Weibliches Bildnis," which I sent to you back then? The reason being that both will be printed by Erwin Löwe Verlag. This is not a sign of distrust toward you but rather a consequence of my contractual obligation toward the publisher that I would like to have my "bits and pieces" with me. In case you would like to read the poems some more or would like to write about them (Dr. Lichtenstein would likewise be very happy about that), then I will gladly send you a copy of the little volume when it appears in August under the title *Die Frau und die Tiere* (*Woman and Animals*). It would make me happy to hear that these past six months have been a good, creative time for you, as it was for me. For I shall express my thanks in advance and greet you

Sincerely yours,

GERTRUD CHODZIESNER

101

August 14, 1938

My very dear Doctor,

Now I am very happy that my fears that your silence may have been caused by something I said in my last letter prove to be unfounded. Please don't worry too much about my manuscript (it's just that now none of the poems can be printed without mention of the publishers; but I am sure you won't be submitting them anywhere anyway); the production of my book is progressing quite well and should be completed very shortly.

But it's not about these things I want to write to you quickly, rather to wish you and Miss Laaser my very, very best. No, I hadn't heard about it for I don't belong to a "circle" of this sort; before I met Mrs. Feld, I didn't know anybody in Berlin at all, and a long-standing, deeply rooted disposition toward "reclusivity" still remains with me even now. . . . This last sentence is only meant as an explanation why I didn't know anything about you but should *absolutely not* be seen to mean that I *wouldn't* be happy to see you here sometime in autumn for a quiet get-together—of course, you will find in me a quite simple, "unliterary" person.

In the hope that this connection will become the "best work" of your life as human being and poet, I send you many regards,

Yours very truly

GERTRUD CHODZIESNER

102

Finkenkrug, October 2, 1938

My very dear Doctor,

Though I am always happy to hear from you, your big excuse that no review of my book from your pen has appeared so far is really not necessary! I am not that kind of person. . . .

Of course, I would have been happy about a report from you; but even if it hadn't been for impossible circumstances, if you, for example, just didn't feel like writing about my book, I still would by no means have felt hurt. I am familiar with your essay, which I own, and I remember thanking you for it and what you said about me back in December when I met you at Mrs. Feld's evening gathering. (But maybe the essay in my possession—*C. V.* 11/11/37—and the essay you mention are not identical). I return your good wishes for the New Year with equal sincerity and then *you* should be the subject of discussion

AND NOT ALWAYS MERELY YOUR GERTRUD CH.

103

Berlin-Schöneberg, March 1, 1939

My dear Doctor,

You may consider me silly—and yet, I must say it because it is true: when I saw your linden trees, I was moved to tears. (And they don't flow easily with me. . . .) Something like a breeze wafted to me from these trees, like the breath of an essence that was friendly and gentle and lovely and no longer exists. . . . No longer exists for me. Many, many thanks.

Yours,

GERTRUD CHODZIESNER

❖

Editor's Afterword

Gertrud Kolmar was born in Berlin on December 10, 1894, as the first daughter of the lawyer and later judicial counselor Ludwig Chodziesner and his wife, Elise, née Schoenfliess. Both families originally came from Poznán and the Neumark and belonged to the educated German Jewish bourgeoisie. Some of the mother's forebears had possessed the rights of Prussian citizenship for several centuries. The father embarked on a very successful judicial career in the 1890s, so Gertrud grew up in a comfortable, educated milieu, yet she seems to have already felt in early childhood a strong sense of alienation from this world. Indications are that the birth of her sister left her dejected and feeling neglected. Gertrud, it has been said, was lonely, and sought refuge in longing for heroic deeds and fantasies about a world like ancient Sparta. As a young girl, she became an outsider, the "crazy" Trude, and withdrew more and more into herself.

At the beginning of the First World War, Gertrud, just twenty, fell in love. When she found herself pregnant, she was forced to have an abortion, and the relationship was broken off. The details of how and when this occurred are not known, only that she subsequently made a suicide attempt, probably late in 1916. Her longing for a lasting love and a family was to remain unfulfilled. At about the same time, she passed the state exams for French and English and was employed in the foreign ministry as a letter censor in the prisoner-of-war camp Döberitz, near Spandau. After the war, she had several positions as private tutor and governess. She also continued to educate herself in languages, literature, history, and other areas. At the same time, she withdrew more and more into a realm of her own, little noticed in everyday life—the realm of her poetry.

She had started to write verses as a child, and her talent was no doubt furthered by the cultural activities in her parents' house, through their interest in music, theater, and literature. Her father, though busy in his law practice, wrote and published several short stories. He passed along the first small volume of Gertrud's poetry to Fritz Cohn, the owner of the Egon Fleischel Verlag in Berlin, where it was published in 1917. She then used for the first time the pen name "Kolmar," the German name of the town Chodziez in Poznán, the place of origin of the Chodziesner family. In the years that followed, she wrote numerous poems and lyric cycles of intensely personal themes. Her productivity intensified in 1927, following an extended stay in France and a vacation course at the University of Dijon and her return to her parents' home to take over the care of her terminally ill mother. In 1928, several of her poems were published in a literary magazine through the good offices of her cousin Walter Benjamin. In her midthirties, faced with aging alone, she entered into her most creative phase. Within five years, she created the great poetry cycles *Preußische Wappen* (*Prussian Town Coats of Arms*), "Weibliches Bildnis" ("Womanly Portrait"), "Mein Kind" ("My Child"), and "Tierträume" ("Animal Dreams"), as well as, in connection with the death of her mother in 1930, the larger prose narrative *Die Jüdische Mutter* [published in English under the title *A Jewish Mother from Berlin* (1997), trans.].

Also from 1930 on, Gertrud Kolmar started to confront in her writings the anti-Semitic invective in German politics. The result was the poetic cycle "Das Wort der Stummen" ("Word of the Mute") and several other ballads expressing her concern with the events. The hymn "Wir Juden" ("We Jews") became her most bitter accusation of the crimes against her people. She adopted a two-pronged approach: sharpest denunciation of injustice coupled with a call to the victims to bear the suffering. In her poetry as well as in her letters, we find repeatedly the admonition for humble acceptance of the imposed fate.

In addition to creating a continuous stream of poetry, she began to experiment with other forms of writing such as drama and essays and the use of free verse. In 1934, a small volume of poetry, *Preußische Wappen*, appeared, and in 1938, shortly before the November pogrom, she gained her greatest recognition in the Jewish press with the volume *Die Frau und die Tiere* (*Woman and Animals*). Beginning in 1936, her poetry was regularly read during programs of the Jewish Cultural Association, where she came to know, for the first time in her life, other poets and artists, including Nelly Sachs, Karl Escher, and Jacob Picard. Even though she was being urged from 1938 on by various people to leave Germany, all plans for emigration came to naught since she would not leave her octogenarian father alone. She persisted in this determination all the more when they had to sell their house in the Berlin suburb where they had been living since 1923 and rent an apartment in the center of Berlin. While most members of the family managed to emigrate, Gertrud and her father remained behind, exposed to the continuously intensifying chicaneries by the Nazi authorities of the remaining Jewish population.

Starting in July 1939, all Jewish apartments had to be registered with the Reichsvereinigung der Juden in Deutschland (Reich Union of Jews in Germany), a body set up by the Gestapo and under its close supervision. The purpose was to restrict the Jews to more and more inadequate living quarters. In May 1941, the Chodziesners had to take in tenants, and in the course of time, more and more people were being added until the living space of father and daughter had shrunk to one and a half rooms.

Starting in the summer of 1941, Gertrud Kolmar and the younger tenants, along with all other able-bodied Jews, were drafted to perform heavy labor in a factory for packing material. Her ailing father was being cared for by an older tenant. In September 1942, Ludwig Chodziesner was deported to Theresienstadt, where he died in February 1943. At the end of February 1943, during the so-called *Fabrikaktion* (factory action), Gertrud Kolmar herself was arrested and, as documented on a file card preserved in the archives of Berlin, deported to Auschwitz on a transport of March 2, 1943. All the tenants who were performing forced labor befell the same fate.

Despite many commonalities between what has been preserved and what has been reported, the present collection of letters brings out clearly the personality of the poet. Her close connection with her extensive family can be felt immediately despite her withdrawn nature and the inner tension between self-imposed solitude and longing for closeness. On the one hand, she closes herself off from all those who do not understand, the "strangers," and on the other, she has a great need to communicate, to confide. It was in her younger sister, Hilde, that she found someone to whom she could open up more than to anybody, as her letters testify.

Her will to serve, as Hilde Wenzel once put it, her sense of duty, and her deeply ingrained sense of responsibility for others likewise find clear expression in the descriptions of her daily life. This is especially true of the daily routine in Berlin, where she was responsible for household chores, except on laundry days, when she was aided by the former family cook, Helene Köpp. But even before, while they were still living in Finkenkrug, she was charged with myriad family duties in a daily routine which she kept strictly separate from her actual activities, her thinking, feeling, and writing. "First of all, it is not customary within the wider family circle to discuss my 'poetic activities,'" she wrote to Jacob Picard. Those with whom she spoke about it were a select few, among them Walter Benjamin. Most of all, the letters show Gertrud Kolmar's personal modesty and demureness, her—as her sister put it—proverbial humility. She frequently fears that her letter might not be welcome, that she missed the right tone, that her writing is too bland, or that she is in some other way not living up to expectations. She frequently places certain expressions in quotation marks to highlight the fact that she is not writing in a casual or self-righteous manner, hedging what she is saying to forestall any possible misunderstandings.

Her effort to modify what she said, her frequent sorting, her sounding out of the mood of the recipient open up again and again an opportunity to speak about herself. As time passes, the letters turn into numerous small essays, as she says herself. Memories of childhood and adolescence, shop talk about writing, repeated statements about her own approach toward poetry, conversations about literature and philosophy become a loosely connected biography which she entrusts into the hands of her sister together with many manuscripts of her poetry and published works. Her mindful, self-effacing manner of speaking allows her also to provide solace and reassurance to the recipient of her letters. When Hilde Wenzel complains to her husband that he is unable to cheer her up, to pull her out of her personally depressed state, he confirms: "I rather think that only Trude knows how to handle this and respond to it."

However, humility and modesty, reserve and diffidence are not qualities that arouse sociability and collegiality in others. She notices this very clearly among the women in the factory and her tenants in the apartment. What she seeks is not casual sociability but something quite different. This something different, of which she speaks with increasing openness to her sister, is love, poetry, understanding of her fate, the relationship to God. "I won't let you, lest you bless me" is the biblical quotation in which she sees, as she writes to her sister in December 1941 and even later, her fateful portion at the end of her life.

Some of the most revealing letters in this collection are addressed to Gertrud Kolmar's niece, Sabine, the daughter of Hilde and Peter Wenzel, who was born in 1933. These letters, addressed to the little "monster," "Püppi," are filled with expressions of tenderness and love and with accounts of the poet's own childhood. Another aspect of the letters is the story of a family being dispersed, of many good-byes from relatives and friends, the exchange of news about the emigrants and their new addresses. Completely in the background, however, seemed to be her own plans for emigration. As to the question why Gertrud Kolmar did not actively seek to emigrate when everybody else, even Ludwig Chodziesner's aging siblings, found refuge abroad, the letters do not give a definitive answer. Gertrud Kolmar speaks several times about the "English matter," which, for various reasons having to do with the unwillingness of the father to leave, was not pursued further. His apparent arrest on November 10, 1938, and incarceration for several days, followed shortly afterward by the order for sale of the house seems to have made him very apathetic, and according to a letter by Peter Wenzel of December 1938, he had given up for the time being all emigration plans for himself, however not for his daughter. Several initiatives were started in 1939 which made possible the emigration of all remaining family members—Margot, Georg, Thea, and Wolfgang Chodziesner. However, none of the pending plans worked out for Gertrud and her father. With the outbreak of war, the situation for the Jews in Germany worsened, and emigration was blocked for the most part. Various plans were still being considered at times until the date of Gertrud's letter to her cousin Suse of October 28, 1941. In fact, it was on October 23, 1941, when the final order prohibiting emigration for the duration of the war was passed.

By this time, Gertrud Kolmar had already been doing forced labor since the previous summer. How oppressive the living conditions had become for the Jews can best be gathered from the stream of police orders and actions put into effect. However, Gertrud Kolmar refrains in her letters from protesting these measures or even mentioning them. Her complaints were reserved for the small group of people with whom she had to share her apartment: a young couple, Rudolf and Erna Berg, the mother of Mrs. Berg, a Mrs. Fuchs, a Miss Meyer, and a Martin Schwarz. They all take over the small apartment and even win over the father with their sociability. Unable to fend off the intrusion of the others into her "only possession," Gertrud withdraws and erects around her a wall of silence—a response often found in symbolic form in her poetry.

Yet, she is not completely alone during these difficult months. She and her father are visited and aided by friends and relatives whose lives are not directly threatened—Peter Wenzel, the cousin Susanna Jung, who is half Jewish, and Hilde Benjamin, the wife of Georg Benjamin. Most remarkable is the loyalty of the former cook, Helene Köpp. In addition, there is a small congenial circle of people who share her intellectual interests, among them her friends Dora and Hugo Horwitz.

The censorship which every letter had to pass made Gertrud refrain from complaints about the situation. Beginning January 1, 1939, all Jews had to add the name "Sara" or "Israel" to their given names so that the sender of a letter was immediately identifiable as Jewish. In fact, starting in 1940, all letters received by Hilde Wenzel bore the censor's stamp. Special events, such as the deportation of the father, were reported in coded form through use of names only Hilde Wenzel would recognize. Peter Wenzel too uses a coding system when he writes repeatedly: "Vati and Trude are unchanged" indicating that they were holding up under the strain, though without hope for alleviation or change. Peter Wenzel is also present when the eighty-one-year-old Ludwig Chodziesner is deported to Theresienstadt in September 1942.

When he pays a visit at Speyererstrasse in early March 1943, he finds the apartment empty. On March 12, he writes to Hilde: "I don't know whether Trude had a chance to write to you before her departure; when I went to the apartment a few days after the air raid, I didn't find it the way it was in previous months and as I had hoped to find it. Even though such an event was not unexpected, the news will be a severe blow to you. But I have seen your and Trude's courage under the strokes of fate in the last years, and I am sure you will overcome this one as well. I am unable to tell you any details at this moment; doesn't matter anyhow."

❖

Chronology of Gertrud Kolmar's Life

DECEMBER 10, 1894	Gertrud Käthe Chodziesner is born, the first daughter of the lawyer, later judicial counsel, Ludwig Chodziesner and his wife, Elise, née Schoenfliess, in Berlin, Poststrasse 14.
JANUARY 18, 1897	Birth of sister Margot.
1899	The Chodziesners purchase a villa in the suburb Westend, Ahornallee 37.
MARCH 4, 1900	Birth of brother Georg [called Junge].
DECEMBER 27, 1905	Birth of sister Hilde.
CA. 1901 TO 1911	Gertrud attends the Schmidt school, Akazienallee in Westend, then goes to a private girls' school in Klockow, Berlin.
1911–12	Attends the domestic and agricultural school for women, Arvedshöf in Elbisbach, near Leipzig.
1913	Studies Russian.
CA. 1913–14	Employed in a nursery school.
CA. 1915–16	Attends a language teachers' seminar in Berlin.
1916	Attains language teaching diploma in English and French.

1917	Under the pseudonym Gertrud Kolmar publishes first small volume, *Poeme,* with Egon Fleischel Verlag, Berlin.
NOVEMBER 1917 TO NOVEMBER 1918	Works as letter censor in the prisoner-of-war camp Döberitz, near Spandau.
1918	Poem cycle "In Memoriam 1918."
FROM AUGUST 1919	Employed as tutor in various private homes in Berlin; for a while teaches deaf-mute children.
EARLY 1920S	Two poetic cycles, "Gott Erhalte" ("God Preserve") and "Wärmt Uns Denken Warmer Sonne" ("Warm Us Thinking of Warm Sun").
1920	Sale of the house on Ahornallee.
EARLY 1921 TO SUMMER 1923	Chodziesner family lives at Kurfürstendamm 43.
JULY 1923	Moves to the development of villas in Finkenkrug, a part of Falkensee.
1927	Employed as tutor in Hamburg.
AUTUMN 1927	Study trip to France with a stay in Paris; attends a course at the University of Dijon.
WINTER 1927–28	Cycle of poems *Preußische Wappen* (*Prussian Town Coats of Arms*).
FROM 1928	Gertrud assumes responsibility for the parental household due to her mother's severe illness; takes a course to become a notary public; does secretarial work for her father.
APRIL 5, 1928	"Das Große Feuerwerk" ("The Big Fireworks") and "Apfel" ("Apple")—

actually "Wappen von Zinna" ("Coat of
Arms of Zinna")—appear in *Literarische
Welt.*

OCTOBER 1929

"Die Beterin" ("Praying Woman"),
"Wappen von Lassan" ("Coat of Arms
of Lassan"), and "Die Fahrende"
("Wandering Woman") appear in *Neue
Schweizer Rundschau.*

1930

"Die Gauklerin" ("Woman Juggler") and
"Die Entführte" ("The Abducted
Woman") appear in *Insel-Almanach auf das
Jahr 1930 (Insel Almanac for the Year 1930).*

MARCH 25, 1930

Elise Chodziesner dies.

AUGUST 1930 TO
FEBRUARY 1931

Writes the prose narrative *Die Jüdische
Mutter* (translated as *A Jewish Mother from
Berlin*).

1933

"Die Fahrende" ("Wandering Woman"),
"Das Räubermädchen," ("The Girl
Bandit"), "Die Ottern" ("The Otters"),
and "Die Sinnende" ("The Pondering
Woman") appear in the anthology *Herz
zum Hafen,* edited by Elisabeth Langgässer.

AUGUST TO
OCTOBER 1933

Writes poem cycle "Das Wort der
Stummen" ("The Word of the Mute").

AUTUMN 1933

Writes the study "Das Bildnis
Robespierres" ("Robespierre's Image").

1934

The volume *Preußische Wappen (Prussian
Town Coats of Arms)* is published by Die
Rabenpresse, Berlin; further publications in
Stomps's magazine *Der Weiße Rabe* and in
the anthology *Das Leben (Life).*

NOVEMBER 1934 TO
MARCH 1935

Writes the drama *Cécile Renault.*

FROM 1936

Readings of poems by Gertrud Kolmar by Erna Leonhard Feld at gatherings of the Jüdische Kulturbund (Jewish Cultural Association).

AUGUST TO
DECEMBER 1937

Writes poetry cycle *Welten* (*Worlds*).

MARCH TO JUNE 1938

Writes the "dramatic legend" *Nacht* (*Night*).

MARCH 1938

Sister Hilde Wenzel flees to Switzerland.

AUGUST 1938

Publishes a volume of poems, *Die Frau und die Tiere* (*Woman and Beasts*), with the Jewish publishing house Erwin Löwe, Berlin; the unsold volumes are destroyed after the Reichskristallnacht.

NOVEMBER 23, 1938

Forced sale of house in Finkenkrug.

JANUARY 1939

Moves to an apartment in Berlin, Speyererstrasse 10.

DECEMBER 1939 TO
FEBRUARY 1940

Writes novella *Susanna.*

JULY 1941

Begins forced labor in a factory for war materials at Epeco in Lichtenberg; from the end of 1942, at a factory in Charlottenburg.

SEPTEMBER 1942

Ludwig Chodziesner deported to Theresienstadt.

FEBRUARY 13, 1943

Father dies in Theresienstadt.

FEBRUARY 27, 1943

During the *Fabrikaktion,* Gertrud Kolmar is rounded up.

MARCH 2, 1943

Deported to Auschwitz on the thirty-second east transport. Since that time, Gertrud Kolmar is listed as missing.

❖

Translator's Chronicle of Selected Nazi Anti-Jewish Legislation, Decrees, Ordinances, and Actions, 1933–1943

APRIL 1, 1933   First Nazi boycott of Jewish businesses.

APRIL 7, 1933   *Law for the Restoration of Professional Civil Service.* Exclusion of all "non-Aryans" from civil service, universities, schools, and so forth. On same date, law passed excluding all "non-Aryan" lawyers.

APRIL 22, 1933   *Decree regarding Physicians' Services with the National Health Insurance.* Exclusion of "non-Aryan" physicians from panel practice.

APRIL 25, 1933   *Law against the Overcrowding of German Schools.* Set up of a quota system for Jewish students.

JULY 14, 1933   *Law regarding Revocation of Naturalization and Annulment of German Citizenship.* Basis for revocation of naturalization of Eastern European Jews.

SEPTEMBER 22, 1933   *Law regarding Establishment of a Reich Chamber of Culture.* Basis for exclusion of "non-Aryans" from art, music, literature, film, theater, and so forth.

OCTOBER 4, 1933   *Law regarding Editors.* Exclusion of "non-Aryans" from journalism.

MARCH 23, 1934   *Law regarding Expulsion from the Reich.* Basis for deportation of Eastern European Jews.

MAY 21, 1935   *Defense Law.* Exclusion of "non-Aryans" from the army.

SEPTEMBER 15, 1935   *Reich Law on Citizenship.* Changed the status of Jews from citizens to subjects.
Law for the Protection of German Blood and Honor. Marriage or sexual intercourse between non-Jews and Jews made a criminal offense.

NOVEMBER 14, 1935   *First Decree Supplementing the Reich Law on Citizenship.* Meant compulsory retirement of Jewish officials.

MARCH 28, 1938   *Law on the Legal Status of Jewish Communities.* Communities deprived of status as "bodies of public law."

APRIL 22, 1938   *Decree against Aiding Concealment of Ownership of Jewish Enterprises.*

APRIL 26, 1938   *Decree regarding Registration of Jewish Property.* Enforced registration of domestic and foreign holdings by Jews in excess of a value of over five thousand Reichsmark.

JULY 6, 1938   *Law on Industrial Enterprises.* Exclusion of Jews from industry.

JULY 23, 1938   *Third Notice regarding Identification Cards.* Jews had to apply for special identification cards.

JULY 25, 1938   *Fourth Decree Supplementing Reich Law on Citizenship.* Cancellation of licenses for

Jewish physicians, restricted to care of
Jewish patients.

AUGUST 17, 1938   *Second Decree Supplementing Law regarding
                          Change of Names.* Jews forced to add "Israel"
                          or "Sara" to their given names.

NOVEMBER 9, 1938   In the so-called Reichskristallnacht, most
                          synagogues in Germany are destroyed,
                          Jewish businesses are ransacked, and
                          thousands of male Jews are arrested and sent
                          to concentration camps.

NOVEMBER 12, 1938   *Decree regarding Atonement Fines for Jews.*
                          Imposition of a fine of one billion
                          Reichsmark on all Jews for the damage
                          done to their property.
                          *Decree regarding Elimination of Jews from
                          German Economic Life.* Final exclusion of
                          Jews from German economy.
                          Decree regarding Jewish Places of Business.
                          Jews were ordered to restore the damage
                          done to their businesses on November 9
                          and 10 at their own cost.

NOVEMBER 15, 1938   *Ordinance regarding School Attendance of Jewish
                          Children.* Complete exclusion of Jewish
                          children from German schools.

NOVEMBER 28, 1938   *Police Decree regarding Appearance of Jews in
                          Public.* Jews were banned from certain
                          districts; hours of public appearance were
                          restricted.

DECEMBER 3, 1938   *Decree regarding Utilization of Jewish Property.*
                          Compulsory sale and restricted disposal of
                          Jewish property.

DECEMBER 5, 1938   *Ordinance Depriving Jews of Driver's Licenses
                          and Telephones.*

DECEMBER 6, 1938

Jews are banned from movie theaters, concerts, lecture halls, museums, amusement parks, sports fields, and public and private bathing and swimming pools as well as from several prominent streets in Berlin.

FEBRUARY 21, 1939

Third Ordinance regarding Registration of Jewish Property. Confiscation of gold and other valuables owned by Jews.

MARCH 4, 1939

Decree regarding Employment of Jews. Introduction of forced labor for Jews.

APRIL 17, 1939

Notice regarding Personal Effects of Emigrants. Lists objects that are absolutely forbidden to be taken abroad: gold, silver, platinum articles, pearls and precious stones, cameras, musical instruments, works of art, and other objects of historical, artistic, and cultural value.

APRIL 30, 1939

Law regarding Leases with Jews. Basis for expulsion of Jews from certain areas and establishment of Jewish living districts.

JULY 4, 1939

Tenth Decree Supplementing Reich Law on Citizenship. Establishment of Reich Association of Jews in Germany as sole representative of Jewish affairs.

JANUARY 1940

Berlin Jews were restricted to purchasing food between the hours of noon and 2:00 P.M.

JANUARY 15, 1940

Ration coupons for Jews for all meat and vegetables were invalidated.

JANUARY 31, 1940

Prohibition throughout Germany to sell milk, fish, poultry, peas, barley, rice, and canned milk to Jews.

FEBRUARY 2, 1940 — *Decree regarding Emigration Tax for Jews (Reichfluchtsteuer).* Imposition of special emigration tax for Jews.

FEBRUARY 6, 1940 — *Decree regarding Clothes Rationing for Jews.* Clothes ration cards withheld from Jews.

APRIL 5, 1940 — Berlin city council limits the time of food shopping for Jews from noon to 12:30 P.M. Later, this is shifted to between four and five o'clock, when the stocks were depleted.

SEPTEMBER 1, 1941 — *Police Decree regarding Identification Badges for Jews.* All Jews over the age of six compelled to wear a yellow Star of David marked with the word "Jew." Went into effect September 19.

OCTOBER 31, 1941 — *Decree regarding Employment of Jews.* Strict regulations governing employment of Jews.

APRIL 17, 1942 — *Decree regarding Public Conveyances.* Use of public transportation prohibited to Jews except to go to work.
Ordinance regarding Identification of Jewish Apartments. Compulsory marking of Jewish apartments with a Star of David.

JUNE 19, 1942 — Decree allowing confiscation of electric appliances, typewriters, and bicycles owned by Jews.

OCTOBER 9, 1942 — Decree forbidding Jews to buy books.

FEBRUARY 28, 1943 — *Fabrikaktion*—remaining Jews in Berlin were arrested at the factories where they were performing forced labor and transported to Auschwitz.

Editor's Notes to the Letters

1
Ella
Longtime friend of Gertrud Kolmar.

working as a translator
Gertrud Kolmar was employed at the prisoner-of-war camp in Döberitz during the First World War.

Brockhaus
German encyclopedia.

my book
Die Frau und die Tiere (*Woman and Animals*), published in August 1938.

"monster"
Term of endearment for Sabine Wenzel, daughter of Hilde Wenzel.

2
Postcard from Ludwig Chodziesner with addition by Gertrud Kolmar.

3
"my" reader
Erna Feld Leonhard was reciting Gertrud Kolmar's poetry at evening performances by the Jüdische Kulturbund (Jewish Cultural Assocation).

Helene
Helene Köpp was the cook in the Chodziesner household for forty years.

the reviewer
Hugo Lachmanski (b. 1872 in Berlin; d. 1943 in Theresienstadt) wrote a review of *Die Frau und die Tiere* on September 22, 1938. The following is an excerpt:

The small volume of poems being presented here permits a welcome opportunity to gain an overview of the complete work of a poet whose path does not get lost in the tangle of the lyrically conventional but who goes her solitary way, real-unreal, equipped with the armor of an entirely unusual diction, whose goal is a mysterious realm of fantastic visions. . . .

Gertrud Chodziesner's poetry contains few deeply felt natural sounds, for the outstanding characteristic of this poetry is the baroque, a language of lavish opulence of strange imagery and ornamental, picturesque flourishes. The poet revels in colors the likes of which can only be found in recent times on the palette of the French Symbolist Arthur Rimbaud. Whatever it was that may have awakened in this poet her sense of color . . . , this sun brown, rose red, this peacock blue and orange, the black greenish and silver colored, this orange yellow and emerald, this copper and gray bluish, it all constitutes the profuse, ornamental accessory to a lyrical language over which vault the boldest, most remote metaphors like a dark and heavy cupola. . . .

C. V. [Central-Verein Zeitung]

Newspaper published by the Central Organization of Jews in Germany, the largest Jewish organization still functioning in Germany; publication ceased after the pogrom in November 1938.

Else Lasker-Schüler

Well-known German Jewish poetess (1869–1945).

Jean Giono

French novelist (1895–1970).

Lindenheims

Rebecka, sister of Ludwig Chodziesner, was married to Alexander Lindenheim. In December 1940, she and her husband immigrated to Montevideo, Uruguay, where she died in 1962.

Mrs. B.

Betty Benario, mother of Ilse Benario, a close friend of Gertrud Kolmar.

4
Letter card.

the "English" matter

Reference to plans for Gertrud Kolmar's emigration to Great Britain which were initiated by Hilde Wenzel.

we sold our house

Forced sale of the house in Finkenkrug, a suburb where the Chodziesners had been living since 1923. The looming censorship did not permit a more detailed description of the circumstances and events.

Hilde Wenzel apparently complained to her husband about her sister's wavering with regard to emigration plans. On December 2, 1938, Peter Wenzel replies: "You're completely justified in being annoyed about Trude's wavering. The children [Georg and Margot Chodziesner] and I were impressed with what energy you have been tackling this matter. Trude will be free to go as soon as Vati will be placed somewhere. I believe this is also what he would want. That is, since February 1, 1939, which isn't all that long anymore. Vati still resists against a private hostel, but that may change. I will take a ride out on Sunday. Your way of handling Trude's affairs is, at any rate, the right one."

On December 18, he writes: "[Vati] has given up any emigration plans for himself for the time being, however not for Trude. She'll write."

In her letters of December 23 and February 15, Gertrud Kolmar discusses her position further.

5
Addendum to a letter by Ludwig Chodziesner.

about this matter
Plans for emigration.

since 1923 or even since 1894
Dates of moves by the Family Chodziesner.

Püppi
Nickname for Sabine Wenzel, meaning little doll.

"Brehm"
Standard German reference work about wildlife.

the Giono
Jean le Bleu (1932), novel by Jean Giono.

6
Addendum to a letter by Ludwig Chodziesner.

Speyererstrasse
In Berlin Schöneberg where Gertrud and Ludwig Chodziesner rented an apartment.

helps me with the housework
Gertrud Kolmar expressed her dissatisfaction about the tenants in a satirical play titled *Furnished Lady (With Use of Kitchen)*. The main character of the

play is a woman tenant of a furnished room who is supposed to help out with household chores in return for free room and board. In her monologue, which reiterates questions, answers, and objections of the "silent" partner in the conversation (that is, the landlady), the tenant reveals her own vanity, stupidity, and greed. Published in Gertrud Kolmar, *Orte,* ed. Marion Brandt (Berlin, 1994).

Bienelein
Nickname for Sabine Wenzel.

Junge
Literally, boy; family name for Georg Chodziesner, brother of Gertrud Kolmar.

Peter
Peter Wenzel, Hilde Wenzel's non-Jewish husband, who remained in Berlin.

7
Stahnsdorf
Jewish cemetery where Elise Chodziesner was buried.

a book by Hermann Hesse
Reference to *Der Weg nach Innen (The Path Inward),* 1931.

Jakob Picard
Jakob (Jacob) Picard (1883–1967), writer of Jewish-Swabian rural stories and friend of Gertrud Kolmar. He immigrated to the United States in 1940 and was the first to write about her in articles in the New York German-Jewish newspaper *Der Aufbau* and in *Commentary.*

Bertha Badt-Strauss
Literary historian and writer (1885–1970); immigrated to the United States in 1939. Among her publications are *Rahel Varnhagen und ihre Zeit (Rahel Varnhagen and Her Time),* 1912; *Süßkind von Trimberg,* 1920; *Moses Mendelssohn, der Mensch und das Werk (Moses Mendelssohn, the Man and His Work),* 1929; and *Jüdinnen (Jewish Women),* 1937. She was married to Bruno Strauss, who taught history and German literature in Shreveport, Louisiana, from 1939 to 1964.

Der Morgen
Monthly magazine published by the Central Organization of Jews in Germany (1925–38). Founded by Julius Goldstein in Darmstadt. The text of

Bertha Badt-Strauss's review for the last issue was not published. It read: "It has been a long time since a book has had such an effect on me—especially in these worrisome times—: an enchantment to be able to breathe for one day and one night a different world, in a strange, magic world replete with hard, glittering crystals, with eerie animals, and suffering human beings. Gertrud Chodziesner and her poems, *Die Frau und die Tiere*, . . . gave me such an experience I haven't had for a long time, which attests to the fact that here was heard a strange, idiosyncratic voice, remote from much of what has been created in our time 'in an educated language which composes poetry and thinks for us.' A boundless loneliness seems to envelop this book. . . ." Cited in *Orte*.

Kanga
Not identified, possibly a made-up word.

Margot
Margot Chodziesner (1897–1942), zoologist, second oldest of the Chodziesner children. She immigrated to Italy in 1938 and later to Australia, where she died in 1942.

Mrs. Horwitz
The painter Dora Horwitz and her husband, Dr. Hugo Horwitz, a private scholar and Spinoza expert, were friends of Nelly Sachs as well as Gertrud Kolmar. Both were deported to Riga in September 1942 and are listed as missing. In the later letters, they are referred to as "close acquaintances," "friends," and the "Westend couple."

8
the *Träumer* you gave me
"Dreamer," German title of Jean Giono's novel *Jean le Bleu*.

"Sechseläuten"
Ringing of the hour of six; a Zurich tradition.

poem by Gottfried Keller
"Wegelied" ("Wayfaring Song") from *Die Leute von Seldwyla* (*The People of Seldwyla*), 1874, by the Swiss writer Gottfried Keller.

my Pegasus
Winged white horse from Greek mythology; here used as a metaphor for creative inspiration.

Weißensee
Jewish cemetery in Berlin where the grandparents Johanna and Julius
Chodziesner were buried.

L's
Probably Alexander and Rebecka Lindenheim.

9
your Greek journey
Hilde Wenzel traveled to Greece in the summer of 1939.

in Dijon and Paris
Reference to Gertrud Kolmar's study trip to France in 1927.

Grandma Sch.
Hedwig Schoenfliess (née Hirschfeld, 1844–1908), maternal grandmother,
who undertook a journey to Egypt, Greece, and Turkey at the turn of the
century. Walter Benjamin recalls this grandmother in *Berliner Kindheit um
Neunzehnhundert* (*Berlin Childhood about 1900*).

her cousin
Wolfgang Chodziesner, son of Thea and Georg, born 1936.

Justice Pakscher
Colleague of Ludwig Chodziesner.

since the Junge is now gone
Georg Chodziesner left Germany in August 1939. In a letter of November
20, 1968, he describes his flight from Germany and his emigration in detail:

> I left Berlin on August 10, 1939, on a collective transport for Camp Kitchener in
> Kent, England. This was a transit camp for people whose lives were in danger in
> Germany and who had prospects of immigration to other countries. Though I
> had an affidavit for the United States, I would have had to wait for two years for
> an entrance visa due to the American quota system. Meanwhile, we heard from an
> uncle in South America that a visa for us from Chile was on its way to Berlin. But
> since I had been hunted by the Gestapo in November 1938 and lived in hiding
> for two weeks, I had been advised by our local police to disappear as soon as pos-
> sible. The Chilean consulate in Berlin promised to forward my visa to their con-
> sulate in London. Since the war had broken out when the visa arrived, this was no
> longer possible. [. . .] I myself was interned on the Isle of Man in May 1940 (after
> the fall of Belgium and France). In June 1940, the internees were sent to various
> countries overseas. The letter in question indicates, therefore, that I was not
> transported to America (Helmut), but to Australia (where my sister Margot was

living). [. . .] In Australia, I was interned and all efforts to immigrate to North or South America were for naught. In September 1942, I volunteered for the Australian army and in December 1945, I reentered civilian life. Meanwhile, my wife had died in Chile, and I succeeded, after protracted efforts, in being reunited with my son, Wolfgang, in Australia in May 1945.

10

Flora
The family dog, a borzoi, which the Chodziesners were forced to give away.

11

a ticket to Chile
Emigration papers.

C. F. Meyer
Conrad Ferdinand Meyer (1825–98), a Swiss German poet and short-story writer.

my Tiberius drama
A dramatic work by Kolmar about the Roman emperor Tiberius.

12

Birthday card for Sabine Wenzel.

by a very old grandma
Hedwig Schoenfliess, Gertrud Kolmar's grandmother.

13

Wedding
Working-class residential district in Berlin.

For out of the abundance of the heart the mouth speaks
Quote from Matthew 12:34.

Thea from Genoa
Thea Chodziesner immigrated with her son, Wolfgang, in December 1939 via Genoa to Concepción, Chile, where she died in 1942.

Suse
Susanne Jung, second cousin and friend of Gertrud Kolmar, whom she entrusted with several of her works.

14

"Greek Travels"
Hilde Wenzel's travelogue.

15

Ilse Benario
Gertrud Kolmar's friend, who was married in the Netherlands.

always at night
Reference to the writing of the novella *Susanna*.

16

Letter of Ludwig Chodziesner with addendum by Gertrud Kolmar to her niece Sabine.

17

Letter of Gertrud Kolmar to her brother Georg Chodziesner, preserved in incomplete typescript by Hilde Wenzel.

"former area"
Finkenkrug.

but so far, nothing
It seems that Hilde Wenzel cut the letter at this point. The last paragraph follows a broader introduction rather abruptly. The typescript gives the same impression.

18

Matischok's successor
Matischok was formerly the Chodziesners' gardener.

Wally
Former maid of the Chodziesners.

Betty
Betty Benario, mother of Ilse. She and her husband were neighbors and good friends of the Chodziesners in Westend. Leopold Benario was the director of the prominent publishing house Mosse Verlag.

"fundo"
Spanish for landed estate.

Uncle Mole
Uncle of Thea Chodziesner, brother of Julius Galliner.

19

This is the greatest comfort
Source unidentified.

"My love, my child, how wonderful"
Quote from the poem "An die Geliebte" ("To My Beloved") by Max Brod, in
Das Buch der Liebe (*The Book of Love*).

A few people are close to me
Among these friends were apparently Dora and Hugo Horwitz.

Buddenbrooks
Novel by Thomas Mann.

20

the position I had in Hamburg
Gertrud Kolmar worked as a governess in that city in 1927.

in Peine
Gertrud Kolmar lived in Peine from June to July 1921, working as a governess.

your apartment on Grolmannstrasse
Hilde and Peter Wenzel's address in Berlin.

21

Suse
Susanne Jung apparently accompanied Gertrud Kolmar on her study trip to
France in 1927.

my Hebrew teacher
Gertrud Kolmar took Hebrew lessons and began composing poems in that
language.

cultural association evening
The Berlin Jewish Cultural Association had a series of events under the title
"The Jewish Word and the Jewish Sound." The Cultural Association of German Jews was founded in the summer of 1933. All Jewish artists still practicing in Germany had to belong to it. This organization upheld a Jewish

cultural life until 1941; however, the aim of the Nazi regime was, from the beginning, the separation of German and Jewish culture. On September 11, 1941, the "Jewish Cultural Association in Germany," as it was called then, was dissolved by the Gestapo.

22

Letters from Muzot
By the poet Rainer Maria Rilke.

a little Insel book, *The Song of the Fathers*
Das Lied der Väter by the German writer Edzard Schaper was published by Insel Verlag in 1937.

Per Hallström
Per August Leonard Hallström (1866–1960), Swedish novelist.

I simply "annexed"
Gertrud Kolmar used the first line "Out of the darkness" to create one of her most beautiful poems.

sub specie aeternitas
Actually "sub specie aeternitatis"—from the viewpoint of eternity. This is a reference to a sentence in Spinoza's *Ethics*.

a quite close circle
The only identifiable members of this circle are Dora and Hugo Horwitz.

Marshal Lyautey
Louis Hubert Gonzalve Lyautey (1854–1934) played an important role in the French colonization of Morocco.

"une société d'admiration mutuelle"
A mutual admiration society.

a young South German poetess
Although unnamed in the letters, it was apparently the poet Marianne Rein, born in 1911 and listed as missing in Riga. Her name appears in a program guide by the Jewish Cultural Association of May 4, 1940, next to Nelly Sachs and Gertrud Kolmar, as well as in a review by Hugo Lachmanski in *Jüdisches Nachrichtenblatt* (*Jewish Newsletter*) of May 24, 1940.

another poem
None of Gertrud Kolmar's Hebrew poems are preserved.

a famous poetess
Reference to a youthful poem by Hilde Wenzel.

worthy of a Bialik
Reference to Chaim Nachman Bialik (1873–1934), Zionist, Yiddish, and
Hebrew national poet. Lived in Odessa, then in Tel Aviv.

wrote a story
The novella *Susanna,* which Gertrud Kolmar wrote between December 1939
and February 1940.

23
Letter by Ludwig Chodziesner with addendum by Gertrud Kolmar.

that young poetess
Marianne Rein.

24
Lavater book by Mary Lavater-Sloman
The writer Mary Lavater-Sloman (1891–1980) came from the Hamburg
shipbuilding family Sloman and was married to Emile Lavater, the great-
grandson of the Swiss philosopher and theologian Johann Caspar Lavater
(1741–1801). The book is *Genie des Herzens. Die Lebensgeschichte von Johann
Caspar Lavater* (*Genuis of the Heart: The Life Story of Johann Caspar Lavater*),
published in 1939 in Zurich.

in case Mrs. L.
Hilde Wenzel forwarded to Mary Lavater-Sloman a volume of poetry by her
sister. In November 1941, she turned to the writer, soliciting her help in
obtaining a Swiss visa for Gertrud Kolmar. These efforts were unsuccessful.

25
Letter of Ludwig Chodziesner with addendum by Gertrud Kolmar.

Meisterchen
Ludwig Chodziesner's nickname for his daughter Hilde Wenzel; literally,
"little master."

one and only Bienelein
Hilde Wenzel considered sending her daughter to her cousin Fritz
Chodziesner in South America, a plan vigorously opposed by Ludwig
Chodziesner and Gertrud Kolmar.

26

Sabine's "great journey"
See note for letter 25.

Julian Green
Well-known French-American novelist (b. 1900); among his best-known works are *Mont-Cinère*, 1926; *Adrienne Mesurat*, 1927; *Leviathan*, 1929; *Epaves*, 1932; *Minuit*, 1936.

Dora Benjamin
Cousin on the mother's side and sister of Walter Benjamin. She immigrated to France in 1933 and later to Switzerland, where she died in 1946.

Walter
Walter Benjamin (1892–1940), writer and literary critic. He published several of Gertrud Kolmar's poems in 1928.

Niels Lyhne
Novel by the Danish writer and poet Jens Peter Jacobsen (1847–85).

"Cornet"
Reference to a story by Rainer Maria Rilke, *Die Weise von Liebe und Tod des Cornets Christoph Rilke* (*The Song of Love and Death of Cornet Christoph Rilke*), 1906.

Lessing's saying in *Laocoön*
Laocoön, a major work of cultural criticism by the German poet and philosopher Gotthold Ephraim Lessing (1729–81).

Geijerstam's *Thora*
A novel by the Swedish writer Gustaf af Geijerstam (1858–1909) of the social realism school.

"Dying Swan" (Anna Pavlova)
Solo dance choreographed by Mikhail Fokin, music by Camille Saint-Saëns, premiered in St. Petersburg with Anna Pavlova on December 22, 1907.

"Antique Epitaph" (Charlotte Bara)
Dance choreographed by Charlotte Bara, a Swiss dancer and choreographer; music by Claude Debussy.

Grete Wiesenthal
Austrian dancer, dance instructor, and choreographer (1885–1970).

Lucy Dieselhausen
Dancer (1897–1927); student of Karl Raimund and Grete Wiesenthal.

Mary Wigman
German dancer and choreographer (1886–1973), the most important representative of modern dance in Germany.

27
Letter of Helene Köpp with addendum by Gertrud Kolmar.

Moles
Members of Thea Chodziesner's family.

went to join Margot
Reference to Georg Chodziesner's immigration to Australia rather than the United States.

28
Letter to Sabine Wenzel.

Aunt Ilse
Not identified.

29
Postcard by Ludwig Chodziesner with addendum by Gertrud Kolmar.

30
Tauchnitz volume of the Conrad stories
A German publisher specializing in publishing American and English literature in the original language.

The Plumed Serpent
By D. H. Lawrence, published in German translation in 1932. Gertrud Kolmar read it in the original English.

Ivrit
Hebrew for Hebrew.

Tchernikovsky
Saul Tchernikovsky (1875–1943), physician and Hebrew poet, born in Russia. Important representative of modern Hebrew literature.

Bosy
Karl Bosy, employee at the Wenzel bookstore. He was killed during the
German invasion of France in May 1940.

Lawrence said in *The Plumed Serpent*
The passage cited was likely translated into German by Gertrud Kolmar
herself. Here reprinted in the original.

toward the East, toward the southeast
Gertrud Kolmar repeatedly expressed a longing in her poetry and letters for
the East.

31
Letter by Ludwig Chodziesner with addendum by Gertrud Kolmar.

Mrs. Lavater's Russian is probably better than mine
Mary Lavater-Sloman lived for some time in Russia. Gertrud Kolmar studied Russian in 1913 and 1914.

War and Peace
Novel by Leo Tolstoy, originally published in 1868 to 1869.

Tolstoy's folk tales in the original language
Narodnye Rasskazy (1881–86) by Tolstoy.

"Hadji Murat"
Short story by Tolstoy, published in 1912.

32
"Three Feathers"
Fairy tale by the Brothers Grimm.

"The Panther" and "The Swan"
"Der Panther" und "Der Schwan," poems by Rilke.

in another letter
Letter by Rilke of December 29, 1921 to Lou Andreas Salomé (1861–1937).

33
Letter of Ludwig Chodziesner with addendum by Gertrud Kolmar.

34
Letter of Ludwig Chodziesner with addendum by Gertrud Kolmar.

great-grandfather Schoenfliess
Moritz Schoenfliess (1812–86) was born in Schwerin on the Warthe and
lived in Landsberg on the Warthe. He compiled a family tree going back to
the seventeenth century.

35
Letter of Helene Köpp with addendum by Gertrud Kolmar.

enclosed my two copies of poems
Reference to a series of biblical poems, written in 1937, "Thamar und Ju-
dah" ("Tamar and Judah"), "Esther," "Mose im Kästchen" ("Moses in the
Basket"), and "Dagon Spricht zur Lade" ("Dagon Speaks to the Ark of the
Covenant").

"on all of us getting together there"
Meaning with Margot, Thea, and Georg in Australia; however, none of them
saw each other again.

36
Buber's *Tales of the Hasidim*
Martin Buber (1878–1965), Jewish religious philosopher and Zionist.

Uncle Max and Aunt Grete
Max Chodziesner, brother of Ludwig Chodziesner, and his wife, Margarethe,
immigrated to Uruguay.

Rudolf and Poldi
Rudolf Chodziesner (1914–71), son of Max and Margarethe; Poldi may have
been his wife.

television
Apparent reference to the beginnings of television in the 1920s and 1930s.

37
a retired district court judge
Name not known.

her caretaker
Later named Miss Meyer, who moved into the Chodziesner apartment a second time in March 1942.

Uncle Alex
Alexander Lindenheim owned a hotel in Briesen.

39
Letter to Sabine Wenzel in typescript.

40
to the mangle
Larger pieces of laundry were taken to an ironing machine.

Busch excels
Wilhelm Busch (1832–1908), German popular writer and caricaturist; particular children's favorites are the mentioned works *Max and Moritz* and *Schnurrdibur.*

Löns
Hermann Löns (1866–1914), popular German writer of regional novels.

Peter Camenzind
Novel (1904) by Hermann Hesse (1877–1962).

Robespierre biography
Gertrud Kolmar was greatly interested in the French Revolution, particularly in the figure of Robespierre. In 1934, she wrote the poetic cycle "Robespierre" as well as the essay "Das Bildnis von Robespierre" ("Portrait of Robespierre").

41
Catherine the Great biography
A biography of Catherine the Great by Mary Lavater-Sloman, *Katharina und die Russische Seele* (*Catherine and the Russian Soul*), 1941.

42
Postcard of Ludwig Chodziesner with addenda by Peter Wenzel and Gertrud Kolmar. The return address reads "Counselor Ludwig Israel Chodziesner."

43
before I leave the house
Reference to forced labor in a cardboard factory in Lichtenberg since about mid-July 1941.

the mother . . . the daughter
Presumably Mrs. Gertrud Fuchs and her daughter Erna Berg.

our New Year
Rosh Hashanah, the Jewish New Year, usually falls in September to October.

44
Postcard with the return address "Gertrud Sara Chodziesner," the same on all following cards.

Leslie's book
Not identified.

Rilke's *Stundenbuch*
Rilke's *Book of Hours* contained three books: "Vom mönchischen Leben" ("Of a Monastic Life"), "Von der Pilgerfahrt" ("Of a Pilgrimage"), and "Von der Armuth und vom Tode" ("Of Poverty and of Death"), 1905.

Margot's birthday letter
Ludwig Chodziesner's eightieth birthday was on August 28.

Thea's brother-in-law
Code name for Peter Wenzel. Codification of names in reports about family members begins with this letter.

45
Postcard.

From Z.
From Zurich.

on every train ride
On the subway or streetcar to the factory in Lichtenberg.

"suffering of that great suffering"
Quote from Rilke's *Stundenbuch* 3, twenty-second poem. Gertrud Kolmar

hints that she is now expecting to be deported to the East. The deportations
of the Berlin Jews began on October 23, 1941.

46
Letter from Ludwig Chodziesner to Sabine Wenzel with addendum by Gertrud Kolmar.

47
*Letter from Gertrud Kolmar to Susanne Jung. This letter exists only as an excerpt
in a typescript by Peter Wenzel with the inserted heading and commentary: "Excerpt
of a letter by Gertrud Kolmar to her cousin Susanne Jung in Düsseldorf." In connection with a report about the deportations of the Jews and the likelihood that she
would be deported herself, Gertrud Kolmar writes: letter follows.*

his brothers
Ludwig Chodziesner's brothers in Uruguay.

48
Postcard.

F.
Finkenkrug.

49
The course you are taking
Hilde Wenzel was taking a course in the development of the Bible.

very well be replaced any day
Reference to possible deportation.

a story by Estaunié
Edouard Estaunié (1862–1942), French novelist.

50
Käthe
Gertrud Kolmar's middle name; she uses it here and in other letters as a
private code.

she quoted Hermann Stehr
Hermann Stehr (1864–1940), German novelist, celebrated by the Nazi
regime. Reference not identified.

Jacob wrestled with the angel
Reference to biblical story of Jacob in Genesis 32:23–33.

51
for the twenty-seventh
Hilde Wenzel's birthday on December 27.

by Victor Hugo
Source not identified.

Lilien
Ephraim Moses Lilien (1874–1925), Jewish painter and illustrator, especially known for illustrations of *Bücher der Bibel* (1908–10 [*Books of the Bible*]).

Professor Torczyner
Harry Torczyner (1886–1973), Bible commentator and translator; lecturer in Vienna (1910–19) and Berlin (1919–33), since 1933, professor at the Hebrew University in Jerusalem.

Thea's father
Rabbi Julius Galliner (1872–1949) was a contributor to the Torczyner Bible translation.

Zunz Bible
Leopold Zunz (1794–1886) was the founder of the Institute for the Scientific Study of Judaism (Wissenschaft des Judentums) and cotranslator, with Heymann Arnheim, Michael Sachs, and Julius Fürst, of *Die vierundzwanzig Bücher der Heiligen Schrift* (*The Twenty-four Books of the Holy Scriptures*), published in Berlin in 1837 to 1838.

from her brother-in-law
Code for Peter Wenzel.

52
rappen
Swiss currency.

the Renan
Presumably *La Vie de Jésus* (*The Life of Jesus*) by the French philosopher Ernest Renan (1823–92).

the library in Arvedshöf
A reference to Kolmar's stay in Arvedshöf at a domestic science and agricultural school. See the chronology.

Portuguese Letters
Letters by the Portuguese nun Marianna Alcoforado, translated into German by Rilke.

the hero of my story
With this description, Gertrud Kolmar introduces the story of her relationship with a Jewish medical student whom she calls "my companion." Like her, he performs forced factory labor.

in a "narrow alley"
Allusion to a monologue in Schiller's drama *Wilhelm Tell*.

53
Mrs. Spörri
Meta Spörri and her husband, Johann Heinrich, gave their support to Hilde Wenzel in Zurich.

Margarete
Middle name of Hilde Wenzel.

Rilke's thirty-first letter
Letter of February 11, 1922, to Lou Andreas Salomé.

Duino Elegies
One of Rilke's best-known poetic cycles, published in 1923.

54
Postcard.

55
Postcard.

Leo
Code name for Peter Wenzel.

our Breslau relatives
Presumably family members who immigrated to South America, according to a note by Hilde Wenzel.

Hanukkah
Eight-day festival of light commemorating the struggle of the Maccabees against the Syrian Greeks and the rededication of the Temple of Jerusalem in 165 B.C.E.; usually falls in December.

56
Grandma Sch.
Hedwig Schoenfliess.

57
Letter of Helene Köpp with addendum to Sabine Wenzel by Gertrud Kolmar.

58
additional tenants
Miss Meyer, who had been living with the Chodziesners before; the other new one is one "tenant Sch.," presumably a Martin Schwarz; Mrs. Fuchs and Erna Berg, described as "mother and daughter," and Rudolf Berg, husband of Erna Berg.

a story
Not preserved.

Trotzkopf als Grossmutter . . . Berliner Rangen
Popular German young readers' books.

Gilgamesh
Epic Babylonian poem, one of the oldest pieces of literature, tells the story of Gilgamesh, a legendary Sumerian king.

Gillgash
Presumably the last name of the maid Wally.

The Shipwrecked Ark
Reference to Schaper's work *Die Arche, die Schiffbruch erlitt* (*The Shipwrecked Ark*), 1935.

a larger work about Jesus
Edzard Schaper (1908–84), *Das Leben Jesu* (*The Life of Jesus*), 1936.

59
Postcard to Sabine Wenzel in Latin script.

60

Pesach
Hebrew for Passover; Jewish festival commemorating the deliverance of the
Israelites from slavery and the exodus from Egypt.

From Margarete
Gertrud Kolmar indicates to her sister that her Easter package hadn't arrived yet.

61
Postcard.

wrote in my last letter about Margarete
The package from Hilde Wenzel has now been delivered.

my little story
Not preserved.

62
Miss Schmidt's school
Private elementary school in Westend which Gertrud Kolmar attended.

I remember a little conversation piece
Not identified.

63
tenant Sch.
According to Ludwig Chodziesner's declaration of assets of September 7,
1942, this is a man named Martin Schwarz.

"among larvae the only feeling breast"
Reference to Schiller's poem "Der Taucher" ("The Diver").

64
Postcard.

baker master Weise
Westend bakery.

65
Leo's letter
Letter from Peter Wenzel.

66

Letter of Ludwig Chodziesner with addendum by Gertrud Kolmar.

67

a day excursion to the Westend
To pay a visit to Dora and Hugo Horwitz.

68
Postcard.

69
Postcard.

Suse
Susanne Jung.

70

five people in our apartment who work in the factory
These were, according to Ludwig Chodziesner's declaration of assets of September 7, 1942, Mr. and Mrs. Rudolf Berg, Miss Meyer, Martin Schwarz, and Gertrud Kolmar.

"I won't let you, lest you bless me"
Reference to Jacob's wrestling with the angel in Genesis.

"Gather the godhead"
reference to Schiller's poem "Das Ideal und das Leben" ("The Ideal and Life").

Mucius Scaevola
Reference to the legend of Mucius Scaevola, who attempted to assassinate the Etruscan king Porsenna in 508 B.C.E. and put his hand into a burning brazier to show that he was without fear.

"What one longs for in youth"
Reference to Goethe's *Poetry and Truth,* book 2, chapter 6, literally: "What one longs for in youth, one has in old age in plenitude."

71
Postcard.

72
the Holy Land
Palestine.

the couple in Westend
Dora and Hugo Horwitz.

my walks so far afield
Visits to Dora and Hugo Horwitz in Westend. Jews were no longer allowed
to use public transportation. Exceptions according to the "Decree for the
use of public transportation in the Reich of April 24, 1942" were forced
laborers whose workplace was more than seven kilometers from their place
of residence.

Mrs. F.
The tenant Mrs. Fuchs.

the young couple
Rudolf and Erna Berg.

Uncle Max . . . to Ilse
Max Chodziesner to his daughter Ilse, who lived in Paris. She and her
daughter were later deported to a concentration camp, where they perished.

and I prayed
Compare Kolmar's poem "Fruchtlos" ("Barren") in *Das Lyrische Werk*.

Amden
Swiss town where Sabine Wenzel spent her summer vacation in a children's
home.

Else
Apparently the out-of-wedlock daughter of Helene Köpp, not her niece.
Hilde Wenzel learned about this after 1945; a fact not known to the
Chodziesner family.

Malte Laurids Brigge
Rilke's novella *Die Aufzeichnungen des Malte Laurids Brigge* (*The Notes of Malte
Laurids Brigge*), 1910.

Perpetua
A novel by Wilhelm von Scholz (1874–1969), novelist and dramatist,
strong Nazi sympathizer. *Perpetua: Der Roman der Schwestern Breitenschnitt*
(*Perpetua: The Novel of the Sisters Breitenschnitt*) was published in 1926.

copying those words
From a letter by Erich Sachs in Chicago, a friend of Hilde and Peter Wenzel.

73
Postcard to Sabine Wenzel in Latin script.

74
Uncle Siege
Siegfried Chodziesner, brother of Ludwig.

Margarete
Probably a reference to sister Margot, who by this time had died in Australia, unbeknownst to her father and sister in Berlin.

75
Postcard. Date according to postmark.

High Holiday
The Jewish New Year fell that year on September 12 and 13. The card was postmarked September 14.

Käthe
Gertrud Kolmar tells her sister about the deportation of Ludwig Chodziesner to Theresienstadt, though she did not know the destination.

76
"insecure life"
Reference to the unpredictability of the situation.

Mrs. F. apparently had a falling-out
Indication that Mrs. Fuchs was forcibly separated from her daughter and son-in-law.

widowed brother-in-law
Ludwig Chodziesner, who had been separated from his daughter Gertrud Kolmar.

she is joining him on October 1
Mrs. Fuchs too is being deported.

77
my solace is Hilde Benjamin
Hilde Benjamin (1902–89), wife of Georg Benjamin (1895–1942; murdered in concentration camp Mauthausen), the brother of Walter Benjamin. Like her husband, she was a lawyer and loyal member of the Communist

Party. From 1949 to 1953, she was vice president of the Supreme Court of the German Democratic Republic and minister of justice from 1953 to 1967.

78

Postcard to Sabine Wenzel in Latin script.

new tenants
Unidentified, names not mentioned.

79

The first sheet of the letter extant in manuscript form, the second sheet with cuts no longer exists. It was probably removed by Hilde Wenzel from the manuscript. Hilde Wenzel's typed transcription begins only after a cut {. . .}, no ending.

"free of guilt and fault"
Well-known reference to Schiller's poem "Die Kraniche des Ibikus" ("The Cranes of Ibicus").

this French quotation
"Quand on aime, on a toujours vingt ans" [When one is in love, one is always twenty].

the last bottle from Finkenkrug
Currant wine made from berries in the garden at Finkenkrug.

he appeared
At this point, the original letter ends. The sentence that follows is in typescript by Hilde Wenzel.

Hilde B.
Hilde Benjamin.

80

"Nations perish, so God may live"
Quote here attributed to Louis-Antoine-Léon de Saint-Just (1767–94), politician of the French Revolution. The sentence forms the ending of the drama *Danton* by Romain Rolland, published in 1899, which Gertrud Kolmar may well have seen in the 1920s in a Max Reinhardt production. She also used it as the motto of her poem "Gott" ("God") in the poetic cycle "Robespierre" and identifies the source there as "Saint-Just according to Romain Rolland."

81

Postcard to Sabine Wenzel in Latin script.

82

"this is a wide field"
Reference to the last sentence in Theodor Fontane's novel *Effi Briest,* published 1894 to 1895, frequently quoted inaccurately: "Oh, Luise, let it be. . . . this is too wide a field."

83

Letter to Georg Chodziesner. The letter is preserved only in an incomplete typescript by Hilde Wenzel.

your actual profession
Georg Chodziesner had an engineering degree and later became a patent lawyer in Australia.

84

tenant Mrs. B.
Maybe Erna Berg.

wrote to the Junge
Reference to the letter to her brother of December 5.

85

Dr. H.
Dr. Hugo Horwitz.

86

Postcard.

the sister of Dr. Bamberger
Dr. Adolf Bamberger was the Chodziesners' family doctor. He moved to Tessin in 1930. The fate of his sister is not known.

not exactly his friend
Hilde Wenzel explains in her notes: "Gertrud was especially annoyed with him because he always greeted her with the same words: 'Well, Miss Trudchen, how is the poetry writing?' She couldn't stand that."

87

a cousin of the wife of Justice Wronker
Nothing is known about this coworker or her ultimate fate. Ludwig Chodziesner started his legal career in 1891 as associate in the law firm of Justice Max Wronker.

"I once *had* a companion!"
First line of the poem "Der Gute Kamerad" ("The Good Companion") by Ludwig Uhland (1787–1862); Kolmar's emphasis.

"Be it as it may, it was beautiful still!"
Reference to Goethe's *Faust,* part 2, act 5.

Bergengruen's short stories
Werner Bergengruen (1892–1964), German novelist and short-story writer. Reference not identified.

88
Postcard.

"lonely, not alone"
"Lonely am I, not alone," quote from the musical drama by Karl Maria von Weber and Pius Alexander Wolff: *Preciosa: Schauspiel in Vier Aufzügen (Preciosa: Drama in Four Acts)*, act 2, scene 2.

Hilde B.
Hilde Benjamin.

a visit . . . to Käthe
Gertrud Kolmar is deeply concerned about the fate of her father since she has had no news from him since he was deported; she asks Hilde urgently for any news she might have.

89
Postcard to Georg Chodziesner, exists only in incomplete transcription by Hilde Wenzel.

90
Postcard.

sister of our family doctor
See note for letter 86.

"the strong are mightiest alone"
Reference to Schiller's drama *Wilhelm Tell,* act 1, scene 3.

91
Postcard.

The Battle with the Demon
Title of a novel by the popular writer Stefan Zweig (1881–1942), *Der Kampf mit dem Dämon.* Zweig immigrated to Brazil, where he committed suicide in 1942.

92
Max Prenzlau
A distant relative on the father's side.

my last . . . journey . . . to Hamburg
Reference to a journey to several northern German cities Gertrud Kolmar undertook in 1934.

seven poems
The first six poems in "Weibliches Bildnis, Dritter Raum" and "Meerwunder" ("Sea Miracle").

Büchmann
Georg Büchmann (1822–84), German philologist and author of the popular reference work of quotations *Geflügelte Worte: Ein Zitatenschatz des deutschen Volkes (Winged Words: A Treasure of German Folk Quotations).*

two pages from my "travel diary"
Two poems.

93
Postcard.

Leo
Peter Wenzel.

his marriage
Hilde and Peter Wenzel were divorced in 1942.

94
Postcard.

"walking on clouds, down in the pit"
"Himmelhoch jauchzend, zu Tode betrübt," popular quote from Goethe's
drama *Egmont,* act 3 (Clärchen's song).

95
Oneg Shabbath
Joy of the Sabbath, celebration on Friday nights.

Miss R.
Unidentified.

Dr. B.'s sister
Her coworker Dr. Bamberger's sister.

Morning by Runge
Painting *Der Morgen* (1805) by Philipp Otto Runge (1777–1810).

Caspar David Friedrich
German romantic painter (1774–1840).

position as governess
Reference to a position Gertrud Kolmar had in 1927 with a family Alexander. The sons of this family remembered the "Miss" very positively.

"The City"
"Die Stadt," poem in *Welten.*

my last little work
Not preserved. Gertrud Kolmar also referred to it in her letters of March 5
and April 13, 1942.

Mr. Cohn
Fritz Cohn, owner of Egon Fleischel Verlag, which published Gertrud Kolmar's first volume of poems in 1917.

evening of "Unheard Voices"
A lecture series by the Berlin Jewish Cultural Association.

the writer Josefa Metz
Born 1871 in Minden; died in Theresienstadt, February 13, 1943.

96
Letter to Walter Benjamin, first printed in Marbacher Magazin 55 (1990) in an
article titled "Walter Benjamin, 1892–1940."

where you are
Walter Benjamin lived in Bertolt Brecht's house in Svendborg, Denmark,
from June 1934 to the end of October. From there, he went for a short while
to Paris. Gertrud Kolmar's first letter must have reached him in Denmark;
the second in Paris. Benjamin spent the winter, until the end of February, in
San Remo where he stayed at the pension of his divorced wife, Dora.

Aunt Clara
Clara Wissing, née Schoenfliess, a sister of Gertrud Kolmar's mother; she
was married to the physician Alexander Wissing (originally Wischwinsky);
her son, radiologist Egon Wissing, was a friend of Walter Benjamin.

Preußische Wappen
Volume of poems for which Gertrud Kolmar found inspiration in Prussian
town coats of arms. The collection was published by Die Rabenpresse in
Berlin 1934.

"Wappen von Lassan"
"Coat of Arms of Lassan." Poem that appeared together with "Die Beterin"
("Praying Woman") and "Die Fahrende" ("Wandering Woman") in the
newspaper *Neue Schweizer Rundschau,* October 1, 1929. Walter Benjamin had
sent the three poems to the chief editor, Max Rychner.

due to the events
The Nazi rise to power.

critic . . . who has been assigned
Not identified.

"Robespierre"
Presumably three poems from the poetic cycle of that name.

97
Letter to Walter Benjamin, first printed in Sinn und Form *43, no. 1 (1991), Erd-*
mut Wizila, editor.

request of an outsider
Not identified; possibly at the request of the publisher Victor Otto Stomps.

three collections of poems
In the case of Georg Heym (1887–1912), the reference might be to one of
the following: *Der ewige Tag* (*The Eternal Day*), 1911; *Umbra Vitae*, 1912;
Dichtungen (*Poems*), 1922.

his is called "Robespierre"
Georg Heym's poem "Robespierre," written in June 1910, was published in
Der ewige Tag.

Leconte de Lisle
French poet Charles-Marie Leconte de Lisle (1818–94).

"Le Sommeil du Condor"
Poem by Leconte de Lisle in *Poèmes barbares* (1922).

"Au Platane" and "La Fileuse"
Poems by French poet Paul Valéry (1871–1945) from *Charmes ou poèmes* and
Album des vers anciens (1920).

"Dormeur du Val"
Poem by Arthur Rimbaud (1854–91), written in 1870; first published in
1888.

Milton and his *Paradise Lost*
Epic poem by John Milton, first published in London in 1667; final version
in 1674.

Klopstock's unfortunate *Messiah*
Poem by the German poet Friedrich Gottlieb Klopstock (1724–1803); first
complete publication in 1780.

98
*Letter to Jacob Picard, preserved in photocopy. First printed in Marion Brandt,
"Gertrud Kolmar an Jacob Picard" in* Jüdischer Almanach *1995.*

your essay about the creative moment
Jacob Picard's essay "Der Schöpferische Augenblick" ("The Creative Mo-
ment") appeared in the November 11, 1937 issue of the *Central-Verein Zeitung:*
"We read, even more, we hear the mythical sounds of somebody like Alfred
Mombert or the great verses of Gertrud Chodziesner, poets of our kind, who
are both living today among us poor contemporaries, and remember that

Dostoyevsky in *The Brothers Karamasov* has the poet Joukowsky say in his unequaled parable: 'Poetry is God in the sacred dreams of the earth. . . .'"

Mrs. Feld . . . same evening
Erna Leonhard Feld recited poetry during the lecture evenings in the series "Unheard Voices," where poems by Gertrud Kolmar and Jacob Picard as well as the biblical drama *Channa* by Martha Wertheimer were being read. This event probably took place during the last weekend of October 1937, either the thirtieth or thirty-first. A critique by Hugo Lachmanski appeared on Thursday, November 4, 1937 in the *Central-Verein Zeitung*.

my concerned letter of the eighth of this month
Not preserved.

99
Postcard to Jacob Picard, first printed in Marion Brandt, "Gertrud Kolmar and Jacob Picard" in Jüdischer Almanach, *1995*.

with the two of you
The second person was presumably Mala Laaser, Jacob Picard's fiancée.

to your reading
Picard gave a reading on January 25, 1938, at the Jewish Central Association of Greater Berlin, of his short stories "Der Ruf" ("The Call") and "Der Gezeichnete" ("The Stigmatized Man"), as well as four poems.

100
verse cycles "Tierträume" and "Weibliches Bildnis"
Gertrud Kolmar selected sixty-four poems from these two cycles for the small volume of poems that was published by Jüdischer Buchverlag Erwin Löwe in August 1938 under the title *Die Frau und die Tiere* (*Woman and Animals*).

Dr. Lichtenstein
Erich Lichtenstein was the editor of the Jüdische Buchverlag Erwin Löwe.

101
Postcard to Jacob Picard, first printed in Brandt, "Gertrud Kolmar an Jacob Picard."

wish you and Miss Laaser my very, very best
Gertrud Kolmar refers to the engagement of Jacob Picard and Mala Laaser.

Picard met the writer and actress in the summer of 1937, but their marriage plans and common plans for emigration eventual came to naught in 1938. (See *Jacob Picard 1883–1967. Dichter des deutschen Landjudentums* [*Poet of Rural German Jewry*]. Exhibition catalog by Manfred Bosch and Jost Grosspietsch [Konstanz, 1992]).

102

Postcard to Jacob Picard, first printed in Brandt, "Gertrud Kolmar an Jacob Picard."

my book
Reference to *Die Frau und die Tiere.*

103

Letter card to Jacob Picard, first printed in Brandt, "Gertrud Kolmar an Jacob Picard."

your linden trees
Reference to a poem by Jacob Picard.

❈

Jewish Lives